Inside Rikers Island

Pierre Raphael

Inside Rikers Island

A Chaplain's Search for God

Translated by
Linda M. Maloney

ORBIS BOOKS

Maryknoll, New York 10545

Second Printing, December 1990

The Catholic Foreign Mission Society of America (Maryknoll) recruits and trains people for overseas missionary service. Through Orbis Books, Maryknoll aims to foster the international dialogue that is essential to mission. The books published, however, reflect the opinions of their authors and are not meant to represent the official position of the society.

Library of Congress Cataloging-in-Publication Data

Raphael, Pierre.
   [Dans l'enfer de Rikers Island. English]
   Inside Rikers Island : a chaplain's search for God / Pierre
Raphaël; translated by Linda M. Maloney.
     p. cm.
   Translation of: Dans l'enfer de Rikers Island.
   ISBN 0-88344-674-X
   1. Church work with prisoners—New York (N.Y.) 2. Raphael,
Pierre. 3. Chaplains, Prison—New York (N.Y.) I. Title.
BV4340.R3613 1990
259'.5'09747275—dc20

                            90-7632
                              CIP

To my friends in jail

All beings resemble the way we look at them.
— George Hourdin

CONTENTS

FOREWORD

Czechoslovakia's President Vaclav Havel, in his speech to Congress this year, said, "The salvation of this human world lies nowhere else than in the human heart, in the human power to reflect, in human meekness, and in human responsibility."

In 1928, Lewis E. Lawes, warden of Sing Sing prison, quoted John Galsworthy: "If I had one prayer to make, it would be: 'Good God, give me to understand!' "

In this little book, *Inside Rikers Island*, the chaplain who wrote it is trying to help us understand something about the people locked up in the jails and prisons of this country in an attempt to deal with the crime problem. Father Peter appeals to our human heart so that we may begin to feel for them and then, maybe, to understand just a little bit more than we do now about the men and women in prison, the many thousands of them who are increasing in number each year. The prison population in this country increased from 1970–1989 by 250 percent.

Change is usually slow. It took us nearly 1900 years after Jesus lived among us to understand and then to act on the matter of slavery. It will be a long time yet before we lose our "passion to punish" and to even imagine, and then to believe, that there are viable alternatives to incarceration for 75 percent of the inmate population.

We hope and wait for a better day.

Father Peter, and those like him, respond to the call of Jesus really to love the neighbor, to bless those who hurt us, and not to live by the law of retaliation. It is good for us to read the words of one who, in his quiet way and with great perception and strength, makes clear to us something of the past, present, and the possible future of men and women awaiting trial or enduring a sentence on Rikers Island. For him the idea that some people are born criminals is a myth. The idea that crime is peculiar to a certain type of person, to a certain race or nationality, he knows to be nonsense.

His book is, in essence, a call to love, to forgive, to try to understand, to let our hearts have a voice. He says: There is no failure and nothing is hopeless for those who begin to love again.

LYLE YOUNG

A PRISONER'S THANKS

Arrested, handcuffed for the first time in my life, thrown into a dehumanizing filthy room, the bull pen, I made my first entrance into a labyrinth of pain, suffering, and surprise.

Friends rejected me. The grief I had inflicted on my family ripped at my heart. My own flesh and blood looked at me with mistrust. The gates of opportunity solemnly clanked shut on my life. Understanding and love were just memories. . . .

I am a prisoner, the extreme product and sign of a society torn with conflicting values. Defeated, I am surrounded by the ruins of my own dreams. My inner world is besieged by the most merciless of torturers—the human conscience. Externally, I am enclosed in a microcosm of the "free" society, where hatred, violence, and immorality are the most common way of hiding the impotence felt by those who face the unmerciful giant: Justice.

Desperate, I search for peace and the remedy for my torments. In vain I stumble from door to door, urged on by an interior voice from that Friend who never abandoned me, the only one who witnesses the remorse that soaks my heart. My prayers are answered: a door is opened and inside there are people who care. They make me feel like a child of God. I hear greetings of forgiveness. This is the door of the church of HDM (House of Detention for Men, the hard core of Rikers Island). A church of love lives inside these walls. A refuge of peace is nurtured by the faith and hard work of a pastoral team of brothers and sisters. They have moved mountains in HDM.

This discovery was for me the entrance to a path of hope and the exit from the labyrinth of hatred. Thanks to the many efforts and wise interventions of Sister Simone, Fr. Peter, and other members of the team, I am now closer than ever with my family.

I was able to be reunited with them after three years of estrange-
ment. Now they, too, are growing with our shared experience.
Through these brothers and sisters I have met a group of wonderful and loving individuals who have accepted me as another
member of their family. This is an honor and blessing for me.
Each one of these friends has contributed with support and trust
to the reconstruction of my life.

Only God knows the years I will be kept behind these iron
bars. But these years won't be wasted. With the tremendous
help of this beautiful team, these years will be fruitful. Not only
have I been helped to survive this tragedy, but I have received
enough faith and courage to try to help others.

I am grateful to God for enriching my life with this experience
and for leading me to the right door two years ago. I owe my
new life to this team, which has been the miracle and guide in
my journey.

Father Peter's memory is filled with stories like mine and with
an endless number of his own experiences. For a decade he has
been opening that door to so many of us, leading us to a new
life of forgiveness, faith, and freedom.

GUIDO ROJAS
Southport Correctional Facility

ACKNOWLEDGMENTS

"Prison chaplains are solitaries, hermits," says a bishop. I listen, but I cannot agree.

Although this is a personal account, my work is not a one-man-show. I cannot let the written word outside Rikers Island take over the spoken word inside. Because this book deals with a collective reality, it must include all the people I am with. It is only through all of us that this book can make sense. I belong to a team. There is Sister Simone, administrative chaplain at House of Detention for Men (HDM). A much larger book would be needed to express the ongoing transformation inside HDM and elsewhere in Rikers Island through the vision and activity of this sister. Talk to Department of Corrections employees, inmates and their families and you will see. If we have successfully offered more than thirty retreats at Rikers, with all the material and spiritual preparation needed to get them off the ground, if little by little we have created a kind of supple structure that permits the existence of a community and a church behind bars, if there is a practical solution that no one had thought of before suddenly brought to light, then it is certain that much of the credit belongs to Sister Simone.

The team also includes Sister Amy. She has been a volunteer for so many years. Sister Amy is extremely attentive to the sick inmates, those with AIDS as well as the others, always ready for any possible way to help. There is Carmen, who works in her quiet way with inmates' families, and Rita, who is busy at a Detox Center but always attuned to the prison.

There are Brothers Pat and Maurice from the Little Brothers of the Gospel. Their willing, open presence has always been a gift.

There are our friends from the Catholic Worker and the volunteers from Brooklyn's parishes in Williamsburg. All are powerful witnesses for our people at Rikers.

There is Kenneth Hoffarth, Director of the Office of Criminal Justice at the Archdiocese of New York. Many times his help and expertise have been instrumental. I consider him a part of the team.

I cannot forget also my fellow chaplains in the prison ministry. I hope one day we all will be one together.

I want to give thanks from my head and from my heart for our team ministry, which is both possible and extremely necessary because the material is immense, the matter is urgent, and it is only when we act together with others that anything can go forward.

In preparing this book I am grateful to several people who were a real help to me: first, to my friend Robert Ellsberg from Orbis Books, who invited me and welcomed this story; to Bill Griffin from the Catholic Worker, who read the manuscript with me; to Joe Cunneen from *Cross Currents*, with whom I had substantial talks; to Fr. Tom Clarke, S.J., who always had good advice; to Joan Marie Laflamme, who copyedited the manuscript and made positive suggestions; and also to my translator, Linda Maloney, who did a very good job, in the opinion of my American friends.

I have a brother. His name is Bill Mountain. He is a Jesuit. in many ways his search for God has been and still is an inspiration to me as I carry on at Rikers. I cannot omit him.

Neither can I forget my far-away friend, Henry Tincq, a journalist at the Paris newspaper, *Le Monde*. He came to Rikers Island three years ago. From his trip a book was published in France that we wrote together. I have benefited richly from his insight.

Last but not least, I would like to give thanks to God through those who are or were in Rikers Island, and with whom I experienced or continue to experience the shining part of the journey. If this little book has a soul, it is theirs.

Inside Rikers Island

1

HELLO, AMERICA

God is lurking in every human destiny.
— François Mauriac

It started in Montreal in 1971. I had a few days free after being released from St. Vincent's hospital in New York. I went for a walk. There was plenty of time, and I had noticed that the grounds of the "Terre des Hommes" exhibition (otherwise called Expo '67) were still open. I was intrigued by a new kind of cinema there: it was in a huge, circular room, in which the viewers were seated in the middle and the film was projected on all the walls around them in a circle. The film showed snippets of daily life around the world. Powerful and gripping, it was poetry, full of force and luminosity. It was truly beautiful.

I remember very well that at a certain moment there were two scenes very familiar to me, but diametrically opposed. On one side was the little town of Assisi, like a jewel in the Umbrian plain, glowing with the joy of St. Francis. On the other side was New York, overrun with crowds, teeming with frenzy, the concrete jungle, crowded with skyscrapers.

I had just spent a very pleasant year quite close to Assisi, at Spello. It had been a year of detachment, a religious time, the period of my novitiate. I had thought happy thoughts and experienced a powerful sense of peace. No, it wasn't heaven, but it was a place of profound humanity and simple joy. It had placed its mark on my heart.

And then, at the conclusion of that lengthy retreat, I came to New York after eight days on shipboard. I love that slow advance, the progressive adjustment to new time zones, the rather clear idea of distance. Air travel is not the same. Indeed, the ship had given me the truth and fullness of the change of environment and it certainly was a change. I had never been in America before.

Now, New York and Assisi were juxtaposed on a single movie screen during a beautiful summer afternoon in Montreal. Here were two worlds that were extremely alive within me and in front of me, apparently irreconcilable, but somehow cohabiting and crying out their reality.

On that summer afternoon in Montreal, another world was

3

also still alive in me whose image would be repeated later in a new way. My memory recalled a week's walk through the sands of the Sahara that led me to Beni-Abbes. There were a dozen of us, the same group from Assisi, during that same year, on a pilgrimage of prayer and hope in the African desert, under a leaden sky. Before us, in the distance, lay a village. Three Arab men came to meet us and, without explanation, asked us to sit down where we were and wait for their return. Thirty minutes later we saw them coming back. They carried a big, carved silver tray with hot tea, sugar, and cups. It was all for us, a pure gesture of hospitality, a surprise of sharing, of broken strangeness, a glimmer of kindness in the heart of the desert. I felt an urgent desire to utter praise. Out of nothing came a gem. This lesson I learned in the desert would recur in the upcoming journey.

And now I am living in New York. I feel the need to escape from the buzz of the city, from its banality and artificiality, to break out of the habitual round, to clear out my mind, to distrust the ordinary. Nothing is ever truly ordinary. I want to be amazed again and again, to cry out of pain, out of fear, out of every loss of life's blood, or to praise beauty, goodness, a way, a certainty. I want to be a sharer in human experience and solidity, in the real hardship of life, and at the same time I want to hope and have confidence in what is to come. But how is it possible to reconcile experience, some harsh, and hope? Should one bind them together because experience is a basis of hope, or separate them forever because experience is a barrier to hope? What would each of us have to say?

I say "each of us." It seems as if I am appealing to or favoring the individual details. But what is happening right now within my soul is the enormous anonymity of the city, the blindness of a thousand massively denaturing, brutalizing forces, ranging from pollution to violence and including every kind of human tedium. This morning, for example, at a slightly less intense level than that of all the other devastations, I had an interminable wait in a jammed subway train, broken at regular intervals by a loud voice shouting at the helpless passengers, "Thank you for your cooperation!"

I have no desire to detail the tough harshness of New York, no taste for settling accounts. Dullness and resentment cannot be a way of life. Everything tells me that that is not the way to begin my attempt to study, to show, to explain. Moving out of the crowd without separating from it, I feel a need to share a little of what I think I have learned, the things I have experienced and that have very quickly become for me an endless place for encounter, for unity and for vital reflection. The right way to describe the density, resistance and profundity of it would be to talk of mystery. So let me say just once, and in a whisper, that the mystery is firmly established in a jail called Rikers Island in New York's East River. I have been a chaplain there for ten years.

2

BY WAY OF INTRODUCTION

There is no wisdom in the church becoming the dull echo of fashionable liberal trends. We have nothing to contribute to building a better world unless we speak in a simple and human way from the heart of our tradition and unless we are serious about the study of scripture and serious about prayer. We cannot be radical unless we are rooted in the tradition.

—Archbishop Robert Runcie of Canterbury

How strange — a Frenchman as chaplain of a New York city jail? A priest produced by the Mission de France and years of close association with the Brothers of Charles de Foucauld? Why? How? A little more explanation seems called for. Here in New York I find myself so far from what I am and at the same time so close to what I have always sought. Only a few months before coming to America I would have laughed at the mere idea of settling here, at the necessary conversion and adjustment. But since Rikers I will never cease to believe in surprises.

I come from a small city in south central France called Millau (20,000 inhabitants). I am the only son in my family and have three sisters. Our circumstances were very modest. My paternal grandfather was raised by public assistance, his own parents were unknown. I have carried that about with me for a long time as a kind of "rupture," and I am still convinced that it bore a lot of weight in my orientation toward prison work.

My father worked as a mailman. Without being exactly anti-clerical, he had nothing at all to do with external forms of religion. My mother was very pious. At the age of sixteen I left school and with my father's assistance found my first job as a night operator at the central telephone office in Millau. So, from the period of my adolescence I experienced solitude, working while others slept, resting while others worked. I had time to read and reflect. All alone there, in the big operators' room at a time when it was not very busy, I was extremely free. Many times I used to go out on the balcony and look at the stars, loving, without being able to explain it very clearly to myself, the harmony, reverence and profusion of the heavens. I could think long thoughts, and it was at that time that a choice gradually took shape in me. Since childhood the idea of being a missionary had preoccupied me. But how? In my dash toward the unknown, my Boy Scout spirit was very helpful to me. I am now certain that my job amounted to a pre-novitiate lived in the midst of the ordinary, the everyday and the first stirring of passion.

During my term of military service (eighteen months in

Morocco in 1950-51, in peacetime), and with the advice of a priest friend, I made the final decision to enter the seminary. I knew I needed a solid basis of study in philosophy and theology, and that all of it would probably take me ten years. I loved the Brothers of Charles de Foucauld, founded by Father Voillaume, and knew their contemplative immersion in the poor areas of the world through manual labor and prayer. I also loved the Mission de France, a society of priests founded just after World War II by the archbishop of Paris, Cardinal Suhard, who formed teams of priest workers in factories and workshops, in hand-to-hand combat with unbelief.

The Mission attracted me and, in the end, that is where I went. It was a question of style, of spirit, of evangelical commitment to the world. Here there was a celebration of the team, the shared life, the living church. There were the pagans, the poor, the world of the "little people." God, others, and the Mission filled our program. I plunged into books and the Christian tradition. I drank in the faith. I loved to pray and to feel myself able to hear everything. Our community used to sing: "The Lord will lead us by the routes that please him." It was all too much for me, but I was caught.

In 1961 I was ordained a priest in the Mission de France at Pontigny (about a hundred miles from Paris). It was at a crucial moment for the church: John XXIII had been elected three years earlier, and instead of having a transitional pope, we found ourselves in the conciliar spring.

I was initially sent to the south, very close to the Spanish frontier. We were a team of three priests including Jean, Cardinal Etchegaray's brother. We did a lot of reflection and pastoral work with tourists, for the countryside is magnificent and very full of people during the summer. I remained there very happily for three years.

From the gentle Pyrenees I was transferred to the harsh climate of Limousin in central France, to Ambazac, near Limoges. It is a traditional, hardworking region, de-Christianized and even anticlerical. The land is soaked with memories of conflicts between the local population and the church in its protected and privileged aspect. We were four priests in a crowded community of life, parish work and manual labor. I took care of catechism, celebrated Mass and the sacraments and was also a welder in a small shop. The administration of the town had been communist for forty years, and it was from here, after General DeGaulle's departure from the French political scene, that Jacques Duclos, the well-known Communist Party candidate for president, launched his electoral campaign.

It was in that place that I lived through what we in France call the events of May '68, with its tumult of the spirit, its elements of hope, agitation, and contradiction which, added together, would leave their mark on a whole generation. There were strikes by students and workers; there were riots. Everything came to a halt. In the United States it was the year of the Democratic convention in Chicago, the civil rights struggle, the assassinations of Martin Luther King, Jr., and Robert Kennedy, the year of the quagmire in Vietnam.

For me, at the same time, there occurred a very furtive reawakening of an old and compelling attraction toward the spirituality of Charles de Foucauld, the converted soldier turned monk who was assassinated in 1916 in the sands of the African Sahara. It was not a question of conflict with my brothers in the Mission, but rather of the disturbed circumstances of the time, when everything was called into question, for me it was a drifting, a slow hemorrhage that resembled a profound loss of identity. I felt a desire to move toward a more contemplative way of life, something that would undergird my social engagement and pastoral activity. I thirsted for the opportunity to take more time for God, to listen, to take a sabbatical in order to turn over in my mind the restless agitation into which I felt myself being pushed and which was carrying me away. I left without rupture, without changing my course, without any essential differences and—I thank heaven for it now—without burning my bridges. I marveled at the acceptance and understanding of those closest to me on the team. But still, it was a departure. I needed a lot of time before I realized that we cannot pull up our roots from one day to the next. Each of us has only one village to carry about in our hearts—all this without abandoning for a moment the reflections that followed me at all times during my journey, my exile, my pilgrimage. Assisi, the Sahara—these would be for me, a little later, like a long pause and a huge retreat, with very good bread and a real spring-water cure. It was the time of the desert, of helplessness, of vital encounter. "Be still and see that I am God" (Psalm 46:10).

I was approaching the age of forty and for me it was almost like a return to zero. Thanks to Father Voillaume I was sent to a novitiate in Italy, at Spello near Assisi. This novitiate included a period of three months in the desert where Charles de Foucauld lived. From the outset, I think I may say that I was overcome by the desert; I was completely happy. We sometimes slept outdoors. The sky had a total purity and the stars were clear. We could detect their every movement. On such nights I learned the voyage of the sky, the cosmic animation of the universe, the encounter between the infinitely small thing that I am and the infinitely great. This silence of the desert was worth the whole sum of recorded music. It restored our internal truth to us. We had some memorable nights of offering and praise, of naked prayer, completely useless, absolutely necessary—the gratuity, the risk, the danger, the splendor of God.

It was there, in the desert, at the beginning of the '70s, far from all the convulsions of urban life, that I found myself being asked to go to New York. It was a question of joining the team of three brothers already settled in Fourth Street near the Bowery on the Lower East Side. This "what do you think about it?" with which it all began, and which I received in silence, as a heartbreaking uprooting, entered into me little by little and became my own. Interiorly, in the desert that was so fascinating to me, I was taking the step, with the calm that sometimes comes after prayer.

Thus it was with this twofold past as a worker-priest and a Brother of the Gospel that I arrived in New York on Christmas Eve 1970, only for the purpose of living in community. My first vital link with America was the melodies of the midnight Mass. It was, right from the start, a bond that led upward. The "gloria" of "Angels We Have Heard on High": what a welcoming present! Sung in this little church on Washington Square, in a packed and united throng, it was still the same celebration, the same festal assembly. Even though I arrived in New York as a total stranger, when I was praying in the church with these women and men I was not completely uprooted. I knew that the task of acquiring the language and learning the culture would be a long one, but there was this much at least: when prayer can flow, when I can have some share in that freedom of spirit that is evident when a man or woman prays, I can affirm without hesitation that I am at home.

I knew very well that I would have to earn my right to live in the United States, but to the extent that faith sustains me, and so far as that which I hold most dear remains living and finds its niche, everything else is finally of little importance, a subsidiary detail. What interests me is the hard core, the heart, the interior.

We were then living close to the Bowery in two small apartments, one of which was our chapel. This was my first, brutal contact with the marginal people in this "monster" city. "You're really in the tar pits here," said one brother. Someone else asked me: "What are you going to do in this jungle?"

It was an encounter with darkness, failure, and death through the lives of most of our neighbors. They confronted us every day with questions powerful enough to deflate the best, most harmonious and assuring syntheses. In that old section of Manhattan, the phrase from a book by a Jewish author: "If God does not exist, what happens to suffering? My God, it would all be lost . . ." weighed on my spirit, as did that other expression of Bernanos: "Human suffering is the miracle of the universe." Although I really do not understand Bernanos' statement very well, if at all, if it has any real and concrete meaning, it can be nothing else but the truth of Easter.

I struggled with the language in a bitter daily combat. Already past forty, no longer able to reeducate my tongue, I have painful memories of the early days. When I arrived I could barely stammer a few words of English. Being deprived of even a minimum of expressive ability as regards the most elementary things, not to mention everything else, living from day to day in a straitened dependence on those around one, with an unmanageable tongue that converted the most trivial encounter into an ordeal, feeling that the gift of tongues is evidently rather unevenly distributed — that it is an experience, like bronchitis — an experience one has to live with, something one repeatedly suffers. There was nothing for it but time, a lot of work, of course, and the Holy Spirit, the master of all things. I think of the millions of immigrants all over the world, people who have suffered exile, who have been uprooted from their lives—and it is not always for the best.

"Luckily," said David, one of the first people I met, "language is not the only means of communication." He was right. Beyond language and our different and very particular conditions, which so often are also our limitations, there is the person in each of us, full of mystery, enigma and history. And words are only the poor tools with which we express that humanity. Communion with the world, the profundity of gestures of sharing, these are very often far beyond anything we say. The best presence is to be sought quite far from its origin, in the transparent message of actions and faces, the reality of what is unutterable.

If prayer played an important part in the life of the Brotherhood, so did work, the manual labor that was both a necessity for survival and also a means of social insertion depending on opportunities, of which there was no lack. All four of us brothers were kept busy. I was a messenger, carpenter, maintenance worker, welder, orderly in a nursing home, and a medical aid in a detoxification center before I finally ended up at Rikers Island in 1980. They were years of apprenticeship in the so-called American way of life, of evolution and interior transformation. The most notable result for me personally would be, undoubtedly, my reintegration into the Mission de France. All this was made possible, of course, by the kindness and hospitality of the diocese of Brooklyn, where I have been living since 1982.

The Mission de France and the Brotherhood of Charles de Foucauld are two different states of life, but each is an expression of the same burning desire for God and the same thirst to witness to the gospel and proclaim it to the world—with different means which, by necessity, do not exclude one another. The Mission is brutal contact with unbelief, sharing the sweat of labor, and the intensity of community life. I believe that in the Mission I have made deep, scouring changes in my life that I never could have made anywhere else.

If, in the Mission, one seeks God in God's people, that means going to meet divine grace in events, in responsible engagement with them. In the Brotherhood one nourishes oneself on God in the oscillation of pause, renewal and self-abandonment. In the Mission one mobilizes oneself, discerns, adjusts one's way of seeing. In the Brotherhood one is permanently detached, somewhere else. The one begins at the boundaries, the other in the depths. The one analyzes what is in motion, the signs of the times, and adjusts its life in response; the other carries a monastery within itself. Undoubtedly I am mutilating these things and cutting too broad a swath. In any case, there is no competition or hierarchy of importance involved. In each of the two groups one finds the same two passions: the world and God.

All my early years in New York were filled with reflection on the bonds between contemplation and evangelization, with the importance of being located within the church, the evangelical encounter with the human drama and its questions, with poverty and the radicality of Christ, with the value of a church that is not perfect and complete but always in the making. These reflections and intuitions brought me imperceptibly back to all that I had begun to see and to learn in my first days in the Mission. The prison only served to make all this more vivid.

Having said all that, I am well content to remain an unfinished product, still somewhat unassimilated both in the Brotherhood and in the Mission. I myself can scarcely sort out the elements in what is, after all, the result of two convergent movements, a synthesis of all that I had always been searching for. I can well imagine that the ways of God, for as long as they have existed, are full of this kind of confused mixture. What is certain is that the day all get in line in order to receive the gift of the kingdom it will only be one flock (Lk 21:32).

Prayer is a vital necessity in prison. If I did not pray, I would atrophy. If I did not have an interior knowledge of why I am there, day after day, I would die. But it is also the prison that speaks to me of the Mission, in every one of the realities into which it immerses me, through the encounter with flesh and blood human beings. At Rikers it has all begun to make sense for me. Now it is time to enter a little more into the details.

3

JAIL CHAPLAIN

The human being is an angel, an animal, a nothingness, a miracle, a center, a world, a God, a nothingness surrounded by God, destitute of God, capable of God and filled with God, if he wills.
— Cardinal de Berulle

One evening in 1980 I was called to the telephone. It was a friend of mine, a Jesuit priest who was a chaplain at Rikers Island. "I have to leave New York and go to Washington, D.C.," he said, "and I can't find anyone to replace me at the jail. Could you go to Rikers to say Mass on Sunday?"

"Well," I replied, "I have never done it. I don't know what a prison is like."

"Would you try it?" he asked. "It's enough if you just make a start."

It is always easy to reconstruct the past on the basis of present reality. I remember quite clearly that, as a young man, I was quite hung up on the subject of human freedom. In the seminary, though I had no spontaneous orientation toward a vocation as a prison chaplain, I was attracted by the delinquent youth among the lower classes. They seemed to me to be an enigma, a challenge. I saw their wounds and it was easy for me to feel close to them. It was impossible for me not to see them.

But it was a long time before all that took concrete shape. On September 8, 1980, after a trial period of several months, I was hired at Rikers. Just before that I had spent three years as a medical aid in a detoxification center for alcoholics.

In fact, I was well-prepared for my entry into this world. I had spent years on the Bowery, in the very heart of the urban jungle. I had had enough time to acclimatize myself to the most idiosyncratic aspects of the American way of life. I had tried to remain there without letting the edge of shock be dulled. I had become a student of my brother who was trapped, in flight, on Calvary.

Oh yes, the Bowery was a world full of ridges and wrinkles, often overwhelming. There was not much to be said; it was more a matter of being there, as a friend, with the marginal means at hand. At the detox center on Third Street the corps of doctors, nurses and medical aids was tied together by a common purpose: How many people have we, if not rescued, at least put back on their feet for a while? I was there, not knowing that it was preparing me quite naturally for what I would encounter every day at Rikers.

This broken world at the interior of life interested me. I met there everything I had learned or begun to learn; it formed a unity, like a block falling into place, or a circle closing on itself. I had tried to respond to it in a human way, as well as I could, but little by little I discovered that it was my priestly life that was wholly engaged in the adventure at Rikers.

One of the first prisoners I met was called Kenneth. I had seen him in his cell and had been able to bring him an orange. It was clear that he had not eaten one for a long time. He didn't devour it; he savored it with a slowness and attention that I have never forgotten. That gesture had meaning. It restored a power and nobility to something we no longer recognize and have lost. Or there was another one, Ernie, in the solitary cell ("bing") of the HDM (House of Detention for Men). Clinging to the bars of his cell, he stared intently at a bird outside the window. "I tell you, when I get out I'll never be able to look at a bird in a cage again. I'll open the door for it," he said.

At Rikers nothing is separate from anything else. I read the graffiti on the wall: "Kill for fun," "God doesn't exist here," "Hell cannot last forever." The purpose of my presence is to make sure that that hell doesn't last, not to make people in prison believe in paradise. That would be very difficult in a place where everything around us vomits sterility and gloom, not to say perversity. But escape is not the way; it is not an adequate response. The demands of humanity seep in through the tiniest crack. I am there to promote and enlarge the crack and, in the field allotted to me, to do everything to help the inmates escape from their despair.

It is these people's patience that strikes me most — the prisoners for whom life is reduced to a struggle with the system, with a set of rules that crushes both person and identity. Immediately upon arrival a prisoner receives a number. At every moment he must be prepared to give his number, to show his card. The whole value of the church consists in telling him that he is not a number, that each of us is called by name, that there is another solution.

My work as a chaplain is above all a priestly service; in principle it is a working at depth. As regards physical healing, we all know there comes a moment when it doesn't happen. There comes a time, even for the greatest doctors, when every remedy, every best effort, even the best diagnostic technique fails. To cause someone to live, to help someone to live a full life right to the end—what a joy that is for someone who specializes in the human body! Which of us has not had occasion to praise and thank, face to face, one of these architects of "rescued life"?

But as a priest I am on another level, in search of a different sensibility, vowed to another frustration, gnawed at the core by a message. I, too, have to contend with a certain type of sickness, at the perilous risk of enormous questions and silences—very often without seeing, without touching, without identifiable result, simply going from crisis to crisis, in silence, witnessing, being present, trying again and again. Awkward, limping, a novice, I show them the keys to open the doors.

It may be that the most everyday, and at the same time the most piercingly painful experience for priests, in fact for all Christians, is acknowledging the distance between what they are living for, what they are actually doing, and what they see around them—their own experience of struggle, of sorrow, of seeking in this world that is "in the power of the evil one" (1 Jn 6:19). It is the experience of the present moment, the locus of multiple choices, of yes and no, pregnant with consequences and with destiny.

And, finally, it is one's experience of surprise, of the manna that comes from elsewhere, of unforeseen new developments when "good comes out of evil" through all the gifts of heaven. Certainly everyone is unique, in the same way as the features of our faces are unique. But I have learned to believe in the "totalizing" influence of that experience. It comes in the desert, it comes in the dance, it comes from fire, but in every case a treasure is hidden in it. To be able, day after day, clearly to identify the stakes and the graces—I am certain that this in itself resembles happiness.

That is why personal contact and prolonged periods of listening fill many of my hours at Rikers. I have always believed, accepted and loved the fact that one of the priest's gifts is that of hearing the secrets of the heart, of taking risks in doing so, and, without approving everything, nevertheless of accepting and understanding it. That is the way of entering, in the name of Jesus, into the gracious and unprecedented movement of forgiveness, that magnificent forgiveness to which I will return later in this book.

It is a fact that some people have put their hands in the fire and been burnt. Others are lost and confused, too fond of the shadow to be able to emerge from it. But in the middle of the dark ocean that one sees every day in the prison, the opportunity sometimes comes to listen to lengthy confidences, to find oneself explaining, from one friend to another, the hard blows and the situations that, naturally and objectively viewed, are simply impossible. All that brings a radical change to one's point of view. I know names, faces, life stories. I do not know the penal population, the criminal world. A priest does not look for an audience, but he has "compassion for the crowd" (Mt 15:32).

I see and have seen plenty of tears in the prison: the man who killed another man who had raped his daughter and is serving a 15-year sentence; another, totally crushed, who begged me to pray for him because he had killed the father of a family. These are the faces that pursue me. They do not frighten me, but I keep them within myself. These are the people whom human law has given up on and plowed under, who have no more chance of rising again on this earth. For them I am a kind of emergency exit, a way to a "somewhere else" that is blocked for them.

This is the daily reality in this "big house." I do not read about it in the papers; it is there and hits me in the face. It may be that I succumb to a sort of fascination before this wordless cry in the midst of what is strange, excessive, irrational and illogical, of absurdity raised to the ultimate degree in every situation. But as a Christian I always know that the gospel has all the power needed to bring about anything in this world. And that is why I very often see that it is much easier to hear the gospel at Rikers than in a rich church swimming in security and comfort, where prayer has become routine. This morning I saw a big sign on the scraped down front of a house in Brooklyn: "Fitness Center. Please pardon our appearance. We are under construction." I had no trouble recognizing that our "fitness center," our church at Rikers, is often rough in its appearance. Is it too forced an idea to want to see it as "under construction"?

At Bible class the other day we were preparing the reading for the next Sunday's Mass. It was Paul's letter in which he says: "You are not in the flesh, you are in the spirit" (Rom 8:9). One of the prisoners shouted out: "But that's for us! We may be prisoners, but those words are for us, too. We aren't some kind of garbage. Or if one of us is, it isn't God who's going to tell us so when he is with us!" Another said: "For society, we are always criminals. But there are a lot of people here who are trying to get out of that with God! An awful lot of the time he is the only one you can talk to!"

Even if all that is far from being finished, even if the truth of my words will pass away, to be verified through the filter of my actions, is all that just a dream? Am I just prettying-up the reality? Is this just a special pair of spectacles, focused to conceal and put to sleep all the evil and distress? If there is always the grave danger of slipping away into facile dreams, still one cannot say that God is not present here, or that no one calls on God. It is God alone who can say the final word that graces and transforms, when everything else has been a lamentable failure.

Being a priest in a prison means discovering the treasure of forgiveness, learning from others who God is. It means talking of God to people who now want desperately to listen, when they never before had or, often, have lost all knowledge of and all confidence in God. How is it possible, in this situation, to avoid moralism or paternalism, even a too-easy sense of power over people, often young people for whom the adult world has quite often lost all credibility? Is there not all too often an invitation to play a role, to enter into an artificial attitude from the very start, and thus to be quickly condemned? Questions arise here or there, in the course of the day or the situation, and with them the developing answers, those I have to find day after day, in the midst of so many brothers who are suffering or broken at the very core.

Reflecting on the word *role*, I realize that I have the good luck not to be part of a system in which the precise role of each person is all too well defined. I have not been hired here to make the place run, with responsibilities for surveillance, administration or even control. In this place full of rules, constraints, answers that often come too quickly, I have the good fortune to be a priest. With anyone who wants to, I can discover that for God there is no essential difference between a Christian who lives outside the prison and one who lives inside. The prisoner, whoever he may be, is a being who is profoundly suffering, frustrated, a "loser." Like me, he has an urgent need to find Life. So if I have to use the word *role*, it may be simply the role of an invitation card, of a signpost, of a simple piece of advice that gives the keys and opens the locks. It would be terribly blasphemous and laughable, here as well as anywhere, to play God, to believe oneself comfortably endowed at a bargain price with the fire from heaven. If my brother has only one way to go, no one, not even someone with a role to play, can do it for him. We can never get to the end of the road unless we walk it.

And what do the prisoners expect of me? Not dreams and fantasies — they have already seen enough of those! — but hope, something more than an excess of goodwill and humanity, something other than what they have already seen enough of. But, in fact, it is not a question of me, but of the group, of the shock it causes by its weight and power. For example, when Jesus says: "You are the light of the world, you are the salt of the earth," the "you" is not an isolated individual. He is speaking to a community, a church. I am part of that light, of that salt, but only if I am part of the group to which Jesus is speaking.

How many times we have talked about that among ourselves here at Rikers! We keep coming back to it. This question is a priority for me: How can a Christian community remain a living thing inside a prison? It needs, not a role, but a group of brothers. Where there is charity, there is God.

Paternalism? Certainly, there is a risk of doing everything *for* them and nothing *through* them. And, after all, one quickly discovers the anemic condition and infantile mentality of many of those who are being helped. I need first to have integrated what I try to say to the prisoners, to have made it mine before sharing it. The evil you are suffering, the challenge you are trying to meet are mine; the consolation and healing are mine, too. We are happy together; that's all that matters.

I am the only one who comes from outside. That is a barrier

I cannot cross. I have to respect their tragedy. Here are fifty people in front of me—fifty tragedies. How can I cross that threshold? It is a great mystery, a great risk to touch others' torment. If they give me the gift of opening their hearts to me, they have chosen me. A confidence is an entering into solidarity and dependence. From that point, you have to use your imagination.

To get acquainted with Rikers I used to go around giving birthday greetings in the housing areas. It was easy to do by getting the daily "printout." Now that is less possible, because there are so many to talk to everywhere.

An encounter cannot be forced. I want them to remain themselves. I never know, from one minute to the next, where the day will begin or what will happen as it goes on. And every day is an event. One tells me that he has killed his child. Another says he stole because he had nothing left. This one cannot talk to anyone in his family. That one, like so many, is here because of drugs.

The first imprisonment is an enormous trauma. The weight of the judicial machinery to which the prisoners have to submit, the hemorrhage of their vitality that takes place every day in prison, the thousand and one stories in which the noise, the shouts, the frustrations are repeated—all of it is apparently there to confuse and upset them. Sometimes it is very clear that in many ways the prison is only an image of society or of the street. It is a picture of humanity with its weaknesses, its potential, its regrets and its desires. Truly, evil, vice, and lies are here, but they are not definitive or absolute. Here, too, everyone struggles in a thousand ways for an elementary dignity, truth, justice. If I were to start from the easy presumption that everyone is rotten and ought to be condemned, that there is nothing here but imposture, lies and corruption, that the enemy is everywhere at Rikers, I would have to leave very quickly, without the least hesitation, so as not to add to the number of victims.

Speaking of victims, let me say just as a quick parenthesis that nothing in these pages is intended to conceal the all-too-evident reasons why some people have to lock up others. The victims of all sorts of crimes, some of which are beyond all comprehension, are the first and most violently wounded. I have no desire to blot out or be deaf to all the cries and bitterness at the senselessness of the injuries, catastrophes and bereavement in so many faces. The silence of misery is always burning on every side, wherever I go. But I will return to that later.

Officially, the scope of my duties is simply that of religious service. But to the extent that the administration lets me enter the prison and interact with the prisoners, I have no problem with the system. The administration has no power to control the dialogue between me and the prisoners. It is in that space that I have my unique place and reason for being there.

Am I an accomplice or an enemy of the system by thus giving it some breathing space? I often ask myself that question. In the eyes and the pity of God, I cannot be the enemy of anything but evil. The peace I am looking for, and what I try to find together with the prisoners, is not the peace sought by the administration of the prison. I do not have a relationship of domination with the prisoners. I am with them in a system which, if they come to express it, with our fatalism toward all others and given the opposition of the races, is primarily an encounter of enormous poverties, a mine field of questions. And they know well that the gospel has something to do with all that.

Should the confidential character of these relationships extend to silence about the violent projects around me, the threats that fall on some prisoners or correction officers? People sometimes ask me, "If a prisoner tells you in the secrecy of your conversation that he is going to assassinate someone, would you betray that prisoner's confidence?" I answer that, first of all, I would do everything possible to get outside the realm of sacramental secrecy. The sacrament is a place of completion, of perfection, not of destruction. After that I would try, in the scope allowed to me, and with all discretion, to consider the possibilities. I would act according to my conscience. I am neither a hero nor a fool. One may readily suppose that I would not remain inactive or maintain a complicitous silence. As a chaplain, I think that there are always ways, without betraying anyone, of preventing some greater evil. But that is only true, of course, to the extent that there exists absolute trust on the part of the administration.

As in any place where there are men and women with their

varied relationships, the prison is a living thing subject to the contingencies of every day. Being accepted or not depends on a multiplicity of reasons that are not always easy to discern. One may never dismiss the impact of nitpicking rules or of suspicion. It is true that there are moments that are hard to bear, even if they are not necessarily related to the harsh atmosphere of the prison. Worst of all are the periods of difficult communications, when one senses that the rules are being tightened, for example after periods of violence or mutinies. There are objective prohibitions that prevent us from carrying out our mission correctly, that is, normally; for example, there is the frustration of waiting for people who never come because no one has gone to fetch them.

There are also communication problems with prisoners, who are not all angels and not all prepared for truthful encounters. Indeed, it is true that often the prison chaplain goes through discouraging periods, when he or she wants to escape, to get back to simple things, to normality, which is so rarely found here. We say that you can only see the stars when it is night. It is true, but sometimes there are nights without any stars.

When I came here I had some rather static ideas about the human condition and a fairly well-defined system of references and values. Without having undergone, thank God, a complete destabilization of my certitudes and ways of thinking, I think that now I am more receptive to change, to things as they come. I am a peasant who loves to see, and has come to value, those who resist. The adventure is a daily one. Unceasingly I am led to the essential questions about evil, illusion, suffering, pardon, the mystery of the cross and of salvation.

The fact of being a stranger, of coming from far away, of having had to adapt myself, of being somehow in exile as the prisoners are, has brought me closer to them. Like them, I am continually obliged to rub up against a strange environment, a culture, a way of life. No doubt with time there comes an acclimation, an adaptation, a greater facility of acceptance. But it is still the case that the prison often makes me think of Jacob's wrestling match.

Every day I have to be able to react to events, to find new reasons for being here, to measure exactly the degree of firm-

ness, clarity and exigency of attitude that is expected of me
together with the priestly compassion that opens them to the
hope of getting out, of being healed, of being saved.

Every day I am reminded of my vocation and of my ministry
as a priest. I have to ask myself continually to reevaluate and
reinterpret the meaning of my priesthood here. I need the words
of Jesus; I need to read and to hear them. The prison is my
place in the world, which demands of me even more that I hear
the word and seek for the means to keep it. I need to receive
the shock of the gospel as well as to transmit it to this prison
population. They are the ones who very often give me the gift
of hearing. How many times have I heard these words: "I thank
God that I am here today." It is they who have taught me the
evil that oppresses, the freedom that is sought. In my soul and
my conscience I could never canonize the prison, but I give
thanks to God for the things that come from there.

Why did I come to the prison, and why do I stay there?

Because it is here that I need Him the most.

The Chaplain's Prayer for Breath

Lord, in the prison I will not survive nor will I progress unless
my eyes find you and rest on you.

Of course, I have the help of some friends, my sisters and
brothers. We share a great deal, and not only our scars, our risks
and our visions. All that is a very practical gift, not only useful
but indispensable. It would be very naive to come here without
friendships, complementary, unproblematic relationships that
are simply normal. Lonesome cowboys belong on the prairie,
not in the prison.

But, Lord, I need the certainty of your presence when I pace
the corridors, enter the cells and receive, day after day, like a
blow on the head, the evidence of evil and of a world in frag-
ments.

I need to believe in you through all that is life in me, so as
not to know the defeat of your absence, for everything here, all
the blows, cries and tears, seems to scream of it. I need your
presence minute by minute. I have tried so many times to tell
my imprisoned friends that freedom, which is such a huge, cor-

rosive dream when it batters itself against the shadows, can revive the dead, even here, when we choose once and for all to depend on you; when we decide quietly, practically, correctly, daily, to be familiar with your words, with your life; when we choose the means to seek you, to accept our waiting, without brutalizing anything of the precious gift, the nourishment that is offered to us. Finally, when you are Master, Shepherd, Friend in our lives, one stage is finished. Another opens to us, like a new universe.

Every day, before going in, before passing through the bars, remind me to take the time necessary to mobilize joy.

4

DEVIL'S ISLAND

There is a desert in Carmel that makes of it a field of struggle. The absence of God must be confronted. Everything that ought to speak of Him is so terribly human that it requires me to dispossess myself of every personal illumination, to confront the ways that his Word takes and that are not the fruit of my desire. That is so similar to what every believer experiences that it is not difficult to regard myself as the sister of anyone else who is in search of the light.

— Marie-Françoise, Carmelite

H uge cubical structures, graceless red brick boxes, miles of barbed wire stretched four or five yards high and electrified here and there — the exterior serenity of the penitentiary complex of Rikers Island is disturbed only by the incessant comings and goings of the Department of Corrections bus or of cars transporting prisoners or employees. On one side it is very close to La Guardia Airport, so at irregular intervals there is the furious noise of planes landing or taking off. Then the walls of Rikers vibrate and conversations stop, for we can neither listen nor hear ourselves speaking.

It is forbidden to walk between the buildings. Security and identity controls begin before the bridge, the one access route tying the prison to another world, in this case Queens. From the first stop onward, visitors have to accept being at the mercy of constraints and controls, state their business, get a clearance, open their bags, and so forth. This routine sometimes takes a long time. It is a necessary verification, it is quite legal to demand it, and it expresses the reality of the place very quickly.

I sometimes see the wardens having to show their credentials to their own employees. In the context of Rikers, as in every prison, this is a very banal gesture and easily explained. Here is the somber monotony of a world created to lock up everything with security, suspicion and certitude, to put everything in boxes and pigeonholes, far removed from every kind of fantasy or initiative. Rikers is a kind of global village, very precisely organized under a mountain of laws and rules, but also designed to be self-sufficient and self-contained. An electrical blackout, for example, like the one that darkened all New York in 1977, would not affect us here. We have in place the means to carry on and survive. In this "total institution," this massive drive for autonomy adds to the isolation. The prison, in thought and action, is truly a distant world, set apart, clothed in armor.

Beyond the prison buildings there is silence and the desert, disturbed only by the passage of cars and airplanes, birds of all kinds, mostly gulls, who are taking possession of the place. They are at home, immobile in the empty space. Sometimes you can see a spectacle as beautiful as it is unusual: pheasants of magnificent color and grace. They are indifferent to what is going on around them; their domain remains inviolate. It is only the people, here, who are penned up.

Rikers Island is a mushroom prison. It is part of the largest municipal detention system in the world. Its mission, according to a Department of Corrections pamphlet, "is to provide custody for persons in detention and individuals sentenced to one year or less, in an environment which is safe for staff and inmates and which is consistent with constitutional and professional standards." When I came here, nearly ten years ago, the number of prisoners was a little more than six thousand, not counting those elsewhere in the boroughs of Queens, Brooklyn, the Bronx, and Manhattan, each having one or several prisons of slightly smaller dimensions. Today the number has almost tripled. Besides the new buildings, the prefabricated blocks are a sign of the overflowing prison population. These are a kind of elongated rectangular trailer attached to the existing buildings. They contain long corridors and dormitories lined with dozens of camp cots. Every building has a name: NYC Correctional Institution for Men, also called C 76; "Women House"; "Adolescent Reception Center," also called C 74; "Anna M. Kross Center," also called C 95; "North Facility"; "East Facility"; and so on. I should not fail to mention the two ferryboats moored along the Rikers Island quay. One is named after the former warden of building C 76, Vernon Bain, who was killed in an automobile accident four years ago. These ferries are the last resort in the struggle to cope with the housing crisis in the prison. They shelter those with the lightest sentences, and those who are already on work release.

Originally Rikers Island, located in the East River between Queens and the Bronx, belonged to the Ryker family, who were early Dutch immigrants. Patriarch Jacob Ryker sold the ninety-acre island to the city in 1885. As time progressed, so did the development of the island. Landfill has more than quadrupled the size of Rikers Island to almost four hundred acres.

One of the oldest establishments on Rikers Island is the HDM (House of Detention for Men). It was built in 1933 and now bears the name James A. Thomas Center, for a recent warden. It is a very antiquated structure, and some people in the Department of Corrections still have vivid memories of the riots that have taken place within its walls. At times it has also had a reputation for extreme severity. The prisoners there are divided among eight large blocks of three level stacks joined by staircases. Completely enclosed by movable bars at each end of the blocks, the cells are just big enough for a bed, a small iron table fixed to the wall, a washbasin and a toilet. There are also the various solitary cells ("bings"), an important part of HDM's function. The prisoners who are guilty of infractions or violations mostly end up in these bings, where, obviously, the restrictions are much greater, especially as regards schedules and activities. They are sent there from all the prisons in New York.

All the blocks in HDM open on a single, long corridor running along one side, the necessary route and place of encounter for everyone bound for the mess hall, the yard, the visitors' room, and so on. This corridor is the town square of this village of 1200 prisoners. It is there that many of the newcomers immediately fuse into one, and where people meet each other, for good or ill.

One finds a very different atmosphere in Building C 95. It is a much newer building, lacking any sense of unity, with long spaces that could easily be compared to the long corridors in the subway. By modern standards of prison construction, C 95 is certainly very acceptable. However, because of the size of its spaces, the time required to move from one place to another, and the number of people there for mental observation, it is objectively more anonymous than other prisons; it certainly demands a totally different and difficult human adaptation. In every way, within the very precise rubric of "minimum standards for the care, custody, correction, treatment, supervision and discipline of all persons held in the custody of the Department of Corrections of New York," it is clear that every building has its own style, tradition, and spirit. Each is made up of a group of imponderables, of a thousand factors inherent in every collectivity, especially what each person, willingly or not, brings to it.

In every prison on Rikers Island, no matter which one, what strikes one first of all is the noise. It is like the noise of a railroad station; more often than not it hits you like a blow on the head. There is the noise of the airport nearby, of the planes taking off, the objects of all our dreams, symbols of adventure, of freedom and of escape. There is the noise of the bars opening and closing, the noise of carts rolling through the corridors, the noise of television sets and radios. It is the noise of this iron world, the sound of handcuffs and of heavy keys that hang like bunches of grapes at the belts of the guards, the noise of whistling and shouting — ultimately, the corrosive "noise" of fixed stares. For, as you learn very quickly here, there are silences that shriek.

Even after all these years, I am still struck by the sight, here and there, of bars that are worn, polished, shiny. They are big, solid things. What if they could see, if they could speak? Just a look, in there, is a whole message. They are the fascinating, obstinate, silent witnesses of millions of longings, frustrations, waiting. What thoughts have met here, and go on doing so! There is no end to it.

In the same vein — though this takes me outside of Rikers — I remember visiting someone I had known on the street. His name was Bill. I felt sympathy for him. No, he was not a prisoner. He lived in Manhattan; he had a little apartment of his own. He drank a lot, smoked a lot, but he was lucid. He said to me one day, "I can't allow myself to hope, because hope is a form of joy. And joy isn't in my nature. It isn't possible for me." And what he did, what he said was the only thing he was capable of doing, was to walk in his squalid little kitchen, up and down, always the same route, so much so that the floor was marked by the path he had worn. His feet had left a trace on the floorboards, a line right down the middle.

There, it was a mark on the floor. In prison, it is the hands on the bars. Marked floors, worn bars, these are the deep wounds of a world that is stopped, alienated, restrained, run aground. These bars, these steps often fill my dreams.

In every building, in the offices of the Security Department, you can find, assembled like a kind of inventory, all the things that may have been found during searches in the cells and elsewhere — arms of all types, sharpened pieces of metal, cutting blades, nails, as well as packets of confiscated drugs, cleverly concealed between pages of a magazine, balls of plastic explosive, and so on. It is a very forceful expression of the kind of aggressivity and despair that can be at work at the back of people's minds in this place. It is hard not to see it, hard to ignore it. But without wishing to minimize anything or justify the violence that is hidden, latent, and sometimes explodes disastrously—there is no communicating the horror, no understanding it, it is literally insupportable. It sums up the struggle and strife in this island which, after all, is not so far from that other island bearing the "lady with a torch," with its message of liberty, the phantom and dream of day after day, night after night. That one word, that simple and very difficult reality of a here and now to be changed, which releases an extraordinary inventiveness, a polarization of energies, of patience, of caring, of extreme resourcefulness, betrays itself in these fabricated, transformed objects which are a real trip to the kingdom of escape, the realm of desire: homemade shields, I.D., the panoply of the C.O. (correction officer), gadgets of every kind.

What holds my attention here is not so much the picturesque aspects, the details, the folklore, as simply this: When it gets to the point that one's head holds only a single idea, and when that idea gathers to itself the whole of one's vitality, that is when the changes occur. Anyone who succeeds in escaping, if he or she remains at large, would certainly be able to witness to this. But in escaping from vain passions and addictions, in changing the angle of vision while keeping the vital spirit and extending it over all of us—I tell myself that if, in the midst of plenty or even in a desert devoid of opportunities from one day to the next, I knew how to detect or bring to birth the primary choice in my life and to subordinate everything to it, then that choice, that act of the will could be an enormous driving force for whatever follows. Then the machine would function at full efficiency. Within my natural limits (temperament, wishes, tastes, background) or those imposed from outside, a harmony would be established. Even the deficiencies, rather than retarding, would accelerate the process, the incarnation of a history. I think, for example, of those dynamite-filled words *gospel, life, child of God.* Americans often use the word *challenge.* There are challenges that are sown thick with prodigies and treasures. There are faces, on some evenings, after some struggles, that tell it all, and they tell their stories at Rikers, too.

Nine out of ten prisoners on this island are black or Spanish-speaking people from countries of Central and South America, most of them without papers. All that many of them have in common is that they come from the most deprived sectors of the big cities, from broken or nonexistent families, from a subterranean universe or one open only to unemployment or drugs. "You grow up too fast," one of them says. They know the street infinitely better than the school bench. Apart from that, everything divides them, to the point of caricature or legend. There are the leaders, those who make the laws, and there are the powerless. There are the whites and the blacks, the Puerto Ricans and the Latinos, those who speak English and those who know only Spanish, those who can improve their rations at the commissary and those who never have a penny in their pockets, those who have families and one or two friends and those who come from too far away to have any visitors, those who can make telephone calls because they know someone living in New York and those who have no one they can call.

Given the rapid rotation of people, a peculiar feature of a house of detention (the median stay here is six months, but there are many exceptions, owing primarily to the overburdening of the courts), is that socioeconomic programs, which are often quite modest because of a lack of personnel or money, also come into collision with a variety of obstacles: movements to court, to the clinic, to the commissary, countdowns, searches, alarms, and so forth. These programs have to be continually relaunched and revived so as not to be pulverized by impossible scheduling, sudden emergencies or a change of prisoners. Everything here is governed by logistics and precautions; *security* is the master word, familiar slogan and imperative of every prison.

Separation, inactivity, and boredom are the law of the society, of the subculture—seen, for example, in the tattoos. "We're all in the same boat," says a Colombian, "but in prison the presence of a stranger is resented more than anywhere else." Solitude is all the more oppressive for a South American because his family is very far away, he has little money, receives very few visits, normally cannot telephone outside New York and often has only

the vaguest understanding of the workings of the American judicial machinery.

Sometimes there is an eruption of racism as well. What we
see on the streets and in the larger society of New York has
very strong echoes in the prison. Being black, being white—I
have learned here what the juxtaposition of those two words can
arouse, the sensitivity they express and how the responsibility of
all of us is bound up in them. But if there is one unifying cir-
cumstance to be discovered in sorting out the precise reasons
why a man or woman is imprisoned here, it is poverty.The majority of those who are prisoners here, whether black, yellow or
white, are the real witnesses of the immense gulf in our world
caused by money. Very often the word that covers everything—
broken families, drug addiction, rootlessness, all the failures of
education or housing—is poverty.

In its report of March 1989 the National League of Cities
tells us that it is much more often black and Hispanic Americans
rather than whites who live in poor neighborhoods. Poverty
among blacks is much more persistent than in other groups.
More than twenty-one percent of blacks in the large cities are
poor, compared with three percent of whites. The number of
children below the poverty level has increased from sixteen percent in 1979 to twenty percent in 1985, and the report calls that
a "startling increase." "These figures and tendencies are
alarming," according to Mr. Alan Beals, executive director of
the National League of Cities. "Such conditions are devastating
for those caught up in them, especially children." Here is matter
for long reflection, and the evidence shrieks when one looks at
the prison. The immediate causes, the not very remote causes,
address the bad conscience of our city. When a crime happens,
it often comes out of a long history which is as personal as it is
collective. The world's wounds touch all of us.

In this rapid and very brief overview of the prison, I have not
yet spoken of my principal assignment at Rikers—the hospital.
It is, at the present time (1989), undergoing a considerable
change owing, as everywhere in the prison, to overcrowding.
(New York City jails are already filled to 102.8 percent of capacity.) The hospital, built in 1932, was, in fact, the first building
on the island. It had a capacity of 184 mental and medical non-

emergency cases, housed on six levels reached by an elevator. Now there are also three large dormitories, which have been put up nearby, and which are occupied only by the sick and injured. The old hospital is inhabited by another category of prisoners—those on work release or already sentenced, who are not ill. That often discordant situation of non-ill inmates is the result of emergency measures in response to imperative court orders concerning the permissible capacity of a space and the accommodation of prisoners.

A special case is Dorm 18 E, where there are about thirty inmates with AIDS, the disease which spreads so much terror, the evil of the century. (There were 3,190 deaths of AIDS in New York City in 1987.) Dorm 18 E has its programs, its treatments, its meetings. There are efforts at comfort. The inmate population changes constantly. The disease has forced me and many other people here to witness a lot of human suffering and dying. For example, there was Nicholas, who said to me a few days before he left this world, "There ought to be something done so AIDS patients could die outside, not in prison. If I had a choice, I'd rather die in the East River, not in here." Being a prisoner with AIDS is one of the ultimate screams emanating from Rikers.

Overpopulation, mutinies, escape efforts, suicides, illness, fights and murders all happen in the midst of the routine and the daily round of the "total institution." Life in the prison sometimes appears to be nothing but a concentration of disasters. Outside, you read prison stories, you listen, you watch what is going on, you get worked up when you have to, but you take care always to keep your distance and your separateness. You clutch at the lifeline. You don't want to end up on the garbage dump. It is the survival instinct of the society that surrounds Rikers Island with a wall of indifference and fear much thicker than all the water and bars around it.

Why is the prison milieu like this? What are we creating here? It is not at all natural for a society to question itself about what it is hiding and covering up. Helping criminals, or those presumed to be such, appears to mean first of all doing everything possible to isolate and immobilize them, to suppress the danger that they represent. The arms employed are distance, forgetfulness and still more forgetfulness. It is understandable. Why look for shadows when there is so much sunshine?

But what happens at the prison gate, at the moment they reach the other side of the bars? Memory does not leave a person instantaneously, as he or she emerges, the survivor of a long or short winter of incarceration. In prison these people have learned something more about the human condition. It is very hard to bury a past unhappiness, to get beyond it, and its traces become indelible when they are reflected in the eyes of others. In Kafka's dictionary, which reflects a world not very far removed from this one, nothing is said about the word *pardon*. After all, society, with its tics and its choices, is all of us. It has the faded, gray, bitter color of prejudice and the spontaneous sense of gestures of rejection. It knows right away how to keep its eyes averted. Health, as someone says, is a state of mind. Sometimes it is also an illusion. The stories that follow are stories of real people.

5

STORIES FROM JAIL

He will open a heart of mercy to the deserters from
the Order, telling himself that there must be terrible
temptations that can provoke such a fall, and that
he himself would surely have succumbed to them if
divine grace had not preserved him from it.
> —Francis of Assisi on his deathbed, sketching
> a portrait of the leader of the community

*E*xcept insofar as one has charge of them, daily life at Rikers is not a matter of groups or collectivities. A quick skimming of the island, a tourist visit motivated more or less by curiosity, accompanied by the best explanations, the most precise descriptions, the exact numbers, cannot yield the reality of every day: the personal encounters with those involved, the eruption of the thousand and one stories of human reality that crowd any prison. I would like to give a rough account of these encounters, so far as possible in their raw state. For the sake of discretion, the names of the individuals have been changed.

Alfred is twenty-seven years old. He has been on drugs since he was sixteen. He tells me the names of all the prisons he has been in. He is worried because he is gradually losing his memory; he cannot remember the names of those closest to him, their addresses, their telephone numbers. "My mother tells me, 'There's nothing left for you now but the hospital or the slammer.'" He has tried to put an end to it many times. His arms are slashed and badly marked. "I even swallowed glass, but it didn't work. Father, jail doesn't fix me up. It doesn't cure me. I'm fed up with this life. Can't anyone cure me?"

Louis tells me that when he was six years old his brother Jimmy was killed by a sadist on the roof of their house. One day Louis met his father in the receiving room of C 95, completely by accident. They had lost track of one another seventeen years earlier. The C.O.s were completely astonished to have a father and son before them. Louis has AIDS, and he talks easily about death. "I wish I could help the others; I think I could do it. I have seen so much!"

I recognize Frank. He had been on the Bowery. He had been
in the men's shelter for detoxification quite a few times. He told
me his story. "Father, the day after my birthday I turned myself
in to the police. I thought it was the normal thing to do. I had
been a fugitive for thirteen years, after being in jail in Colorado
for robbing a taxi driver. I wanted to put some order in my life."

Two prisoners are talking. One says to the other: "I am a
criminal. I can accuse myself of a lot of things. They have already
punished me a lot and taken away a lot, but there is still something left that helps me go on living, and that is my wife's love."
He speaks warmly, with confidence, he is enjoying himself. A
few minutes later he is talking to his wife on the telephone. She
tells him suddenly that it is all over between them; she even lets
him listen to her lover, who is on the line with her. Her husband's dumfounded response: "But I'm not a child any more!
I'm your husband!" Two hours later they find him in the show-
ers, trying to hang himself. He is rescued at the last minute.

"Father, my brother died in prison. Now it's my turn to be
here at Rikers." His story could fill a book. Bob has been here
several months while they discuss his case. He comes from Alba-
nia. When the country went communist, his whole family was
put in a concentration camp. After the father's death they let
the rest of the family out of the camp. They had no place to go.
They took to the road with a wheelbarrow.
    They found some construction work. He, his mother and his
brother all helped carry cement. After a few months they were
arrested again. Some sabotage had been done in a government
building and hostages were being taken. After furtive farewells
to his mother and brother, Bob managed to flee the camp, where
he said he had been tortured. "For me, Rikers is a paradise. I

have been tied up, immobilized for hours in the hot sun. They burned me with magnifying glasses."

He shows me his scars, tells me about all his wanderings in Europe, his many wild adventures in crossing various borders, the American consulate in Austria, the year when he came to America. He had a lot of different jobs up to the day when he was able to work in construction again. He stayed in the same place, at the same job for thirteen years. He was happy, got married, had four children. But then came a new snag, a new misfortune. In 1980 the house they had patiently built for themselves burned down. In 1981 his little daughter fell under the wheels of a car. The doctor gave her no chance. She was in intensive care for eleven days and then—she recovered. Everyone called it a miracle.

In 1984 Bob was arrested. He had gotten involved in some drug dealing and was sentenced to a minimum of fifteen years. His so-called accomplice, also at Rikers, told me before a witness that Bob was innocent and incriminated himself instead. Bob thought he could make use of that to appeal his case. But he couldn't, because he had no money to hire a lawyer. All he had was a court-appointed legal aid person. Bob is upstate now, serving his sentence. He has a magnificent family; they are always at our retreats, all four children and their mother. How many times has he asked me: "Why did all this happen? How can I forget? How can I forgive?"

I meet Ralph, who has been on drugs for thirteen years. He is twenty-eight years old. He feels as if his head is bursting; he wants to see a psychiatrist. He has no friends. He has been married three times, has five children. No one wants to have any more to do with him. He doesn't know what to do, whom to turn to. He wants to pray. He asks me how.

A woman employee is walking down the long corridor at the Anna M. Kross Center. She is an electrician in overalls. She is carrying long, heavy pipes on her shoulder, and is escorted, according to regulation, by a guard. The rules oblige him to accompany her, but not to help her. Thus, he walks alongside, empty-handed. The prisoners look on and laugh.

John says: "I don't understand why they talk about the Father in the Bible. My father is here at Rikers. I have a brother here, too. My other two brothers are in the army. My mother's gone. And my father accused me of murder to protect my brother from being convicted. I'm the one who has everything to forgive."

His head is almost invisible under the bandages. They have just removed one of his eyes. It was a prison brawl. "I wanted to start over from scratch," Greg says to me, "to make a complete new beginning." And I have been thinking this evening: "My brother, we are all born old. Youth is ahead of us. Life is just the time given us to prepare for it."

Tony has tattoos all over his body. He wants to see me, wants to pray. "I was born in Dannemora prison, up near the Canadian border," he says, "because my mother was already in prison herself. She was scrubbing the floor when I was born. I was raised by my grandmother for ten years. Later, I ran away from home when my father was trying to rape my sister. I sold perfume on the street. I would like to be a priest. What do I have to do?"

Hal is afraid. They have already broken into his cell twice, torn it up, stolen his things. He was imprudent enough to voice his approval of a C.O.'s decision regarding the telephone. There are one or two phones at each corner of the cell block for the inmates' use. In principle they are free to communicate with the outside since they are still awaiting trial and so are "presumed innocent." So all day long, at least during the designated hours, you can see a group waiting in every block. They are more or less nervous, more or less patient. It is a place that is very susceptible to conflicts, sometimes serious wounds and even death. On this particular morning a hysterical, enraged inmate had pulled the phone out of the wall. And Hal made it worse by saying in front of the C.O., "Now we're all in a fix because of that idiot." A mortal sin. Hal has not been here very long; he is a lamb among wolves and doesn't know that the "idiot" is a leader in the block. It is literally a life or death matter for Hal. Now he is a threatened man, a man in terror. Because there are witnesses, because a captain was passing by, he is transferred to another block.

Here is a man sitting down, exhausted and dejected. "What good is praying? What good is God? I don't hear him. I've lost six years. They say I'm a 'victim of circumstances.' I'm in here for homicide, but all the same. The guy who could have told exactly what happened didn't talk. Now I'm fifty-five years old and there's nothing left for me. What good is praying?"

Eight years ago Ted had a flourishing business. He was happily married and the father of a family. He owned two buildings. But the part of town where he lived was not exactly the most peaceful. One day a "messenger" came to see him, demanding regular payments and threatening difficulties if he should refuse. Ted listened but did not flinch. And that was the beginning of a long story.

One day his children were beaten on the street. Another time his wife was attacked. Somebody threw bricks at him from the roof next door. Ted found himself caught in a vice, with no chance to escape. Too much was at stake: his family, his property. Ted was irritated, angry, at his wits' end. One day he confronted the "messenger" who had come to renew the extortion demand. He took justice into his own hands and killed him. Ted was arrested and freed on $15,000 bond. He was in too much danger in New York, so he lost no time in taking his pregnant wife and three children, finding a hiding place for them in the Western states, liquidating his business affairs as best he could and returning to his native country in Europe.

When his case was called for trial, Ted was in Europe, a fugitive from the law. After seven years, far from his family and unhappy about the whole thing, he returned to New York, ready to face anything so long as he could be reunited with his children some day. Now Ted is at Rikers. His wife is still in the West. She lives on the sixth floor of a walk-up, in a one-room flat with the four children. She has no more resources and is living on welfare. Everything they had has gone for living expenses and lawyers' fees. Ted lives in agony. The parish in New York where he used to live has done everything to try to find witnesses who can bring about his release. But after eight years, the trail is cold.

Ted is pale, a figure of suffering. He says: "When I think that I am in here with the kind of people who smashed everything in my life!"

He is nineteen years old. "Maybe it's a sin to be born. What good is living?" he says to me.

Ronnie's aunt is a religious sister. He tells me that she is the superior of a convent not far from New York. Since he is not sure of the exact address, Ronnie asks me to phone her, to tell her where he is. When I get home that evening, I find the number in the archdiocesan telephone directory and make contact with the sister. She reacts with surprise, astonishment, panic. She begs me under no circumstances to give her address and telephone number to her nephew. "Just tell him I'll write to him. . . ."

John escaped from a prison outside of New York. His wife, Linda, died while he was at Rikers. We—the Sisters of the Gospel and I—knew her very well, admired her, celebrated the eucharist with her in her sickroom. In her poverty and suffering she retained a dignity and simplicity that deeply touched all of us. Even though she was dying, she still found kind words for other people. Sister Simone's mother was sick, and Linda kept asking about her. Her passing really marked all of us. The woman who is now taking care of the two children, while John remains a fugitive, and who looked after them while Linda was sick, is turning them against their father. She doesn't want him to see them. "If you come here, I'll call the police," she says. John is broken; he phones us again and again. He has nobody left in the world. Finally he gives himself up to the police.

Some friends of mine in France send me a packet of letters from children. It is Christmas. They are for the prisoners. Their catechism class wanted to write to the inmates at Rikers. At our Bible circle on Thursday I translate the letters, which are written in French, for the thirty or so men present. Their eyes shine; they are extremely attentive. When I finish there is a long silence, then applause.

A C.O. comes back from court. He tells us about it. The accused was an old man of seventy-nine. The judge sentenced him to twelve years. The old man's reaction: "But I'll never make it. It's too much!" The judge's response: "No sweat. Do what you can."

"I'm not a believer," says Chris, "and here I am talking to you. If my mother heard about it, she'd call the police to see if it's true. I think I know that I have a heart, but I don't know where it is. I'm tired."

He comes from Peru. He is an immigrant, without papers. There is a grill between us. We talk between the bars.

"I am an American Catholic. My family is in Peru — my father, my mother. They are very poor. When I earn a hundred dollars a week here, I send them eighty dollars. Eighty dollars is a fortune down there. The other twenty is for me, for food and everything. I think of them a lot. I write a lot. One day I stole something. That's why I am here. I had nothing left. I think God understands. When the Challenger exploded, the others will tell you that I took it badly. I cried. It's the truth, I did. I could see that teacher, her family, all the children who were watching, the other astronauts. . . . They talk about the end of the world. . . . There's too much going on, too much injustice, poverty, impossible situations."

The shuttle catastrophe had occurred on Tuesday of that week, January 28, 1986. Everybody had a reaction to it, even at Rikers. One vivid impression remains: That same evening there was a television interview with the mayor of New York. When asked about his reaction to what has just happened, he speaks of the tragedy, mentions the victims, expresses nicely, with delicacy, the sympathy felt by everyone at that moment. The shock is very fresh, still burning. His words are the voice of everyone. Immediately following, without even a commercial break, there is another question for the mayor on a completely different subject, a financial scandal in Queens involving the Democratic borough president. At a stroke the whole tone changes. A completely different mayor enters the arena, defending his ideas with fire and conviction, a fighter in grand form who knows where to land his punches. In four short minutes we have two different subjects and two different men. The contrast is astonishing. No doubt a public person, at the mercy of every kind of question, cannot help giving such an impression. But I cannot help noticing how short our attention span is, the natural weakness of our amazement. It seems to me that the speed of reality and its impact on our lives resemble the white crests of the waves at sea, passing over and wiping out one another. My simple Peruvian prisoner, without big words, gestures or power, reminds me of this truth. I have learned something, especially from his silence, and the mystery of this place in which we find ourselves and which we are trying to understand.

Jerry has just been arrested. He is twenty-three years old. He has not seen his father since he was ten. That fact haunts him. He wanted to see him; he looked for him. Finally he found his address and presented himself, "Hi, Dad, I'm your son!" "What? Get out of here and never come back! I don't want to see you." Jerry says, "So I walked out and said to myself: 'The hell with it! I don't care. I don't need a father!' "

Luis is very sweet, very sick, very scarred. His body is swollen, his face gray. He has spent twenty-one years in prison and eleven on the streets, sleeping under porches or in abandoned houses. "I would have liked to get married," he says, "but for a man like me, it's impossible. The family wouldn't have held together. My wife wouldn't have been happy. I have always lived in two opposite worlds: either I was being helped with everything, people saw to it that I had something to eat and a place to sleep, the way it is here in the prison, or else I was entirely left to myself. I am afraid of myself; I don't know how to live in society. I have never been loved. I can't remember ever having been happy in my life. I don't know what it is."

The Bible circle meets in the large chapel. Everyone is seated in groups. The atmosphere is peaceful, simple and attentive.

There are about thirty of us. The door slams open. A captain enters with about fifteen visitors, all impeccably dressed, on a tour. Looks are exchanged. Not a word is said; nobody changes expression. I have a physical impression of being in a zoo. We are the animals on exhibit.

He has come back from upstate and is staying at the HDM during a supplementary court proceeding. He says, "I'm from Attica. I got twenty-five years. My wife and three kids are going to see the psychiatrist. They can't handle any more."

He is sweeping the corridor. He stops me. We talk. "Prayer gives me more rest than sleep does," he tells me.

At the time of the earthquake in Mexico, a C.O. says: "Here in New York we have practically no natural disasters. We only have human disasters. They're called 'Rikers Island'!" And a prisoner remarks to me: "What if that happened to us, that the walls would fall on us?"

Bill is twenty-eight. "If my brother came here this minute you wouldn't be able to tell which of us is which. We are identical twins. Only my brother would never come here. He would be too embarrassed. He is a police officer and I am in prison. I am the black sheep of the family."

Ash Wednesday, 1989. It had been arranged with the Deputy for Programs that we would have a celebration in the chapel today, with distribution of ashes. Everyone is invited to the HDM, even those in the hospital, if they can come. Some people from the outside have volunteered to participate. We have spent a lot of time getting ready. The prisoners know, and they are looking forward to coming. But on that very day, early in the morning, there is a red alarm on the island. That means there has been an escape attempt; this time it is in the adolescents' building, C 74. So everything stops. No movement allowed. As a result, the celebration is reduced to a minimum, two hours late, with no outside participants.

Two death notices come in one day. It is normally the chaplain's job to carry the news—never by telephone, always in person—either to the prisoner, if it is one of his or her relatives, or to the family if it is a prisoner who has died. In the latter case, which may happen at any hour of the day or night, the chaplain is always accompanied by two correctional officers in civilian clothes. Several times it has taken a whole night. It is never easy, never a simple matter, especially in cases of suicide. In ten years I have seen more than eighty suicides at Rikers.

So, on this particular day, I had two death notices. The first was that of a father murdered on the street, but the family asked that the son, who was at Rikers, not come to the funeral. Legally, every prisoner who has not yet been tried has the right to be present at the funeral or the wake of a close relative. The family's reason in this case was that they did not want him to be seen coming from the prison in handcuffs.

The second case was that of the brother of a prisoner, who also had been killed near his home in the early morning hours. There were three sons in the family, the one who had just died and two others in prison, one at Rikers and the other at Fishkill, upstate. "It's hard to swallow," is all the man at Rikers says.

I receive all of that, I listen, I am numb. Everything stops, becomes unreal, senseless. Where am I? What kind of world am I dealing with? There is always this nausea.

"Quick, tell me about God, tell me anything, but talk to me about God!" This worker in the prison hospital wants God as one wants air, light, sun, because he can't go on any more.

In six months Roberto has been taken to court sixteen times. That means getting up at five in the morning, returning late in the evening, and going through all sorts of procedures, not the least of which is being kept in the overcrowded bull pen. Each time, it is for nothing. He has never seen or been able to talk with his lawyer. Every time it is a day lost, full of tension, fear and frustration. He collapses and bursts into tears.

"I wrote a letter to my son," says Eddie. "He's fourteen. The letter was returned to me, unopened, and he had written on it with his own hand: 'Moved. No longer at this address.' I'll tell you, prison can never punish me anywhere near as much as what has happened between me and my son!"

A social worker has come with Nelson's two children. This was made possible only with quite a bit of effort and under strict control, because Nelson is in prison and his children are in a foster home. The social worker, after waiting two hours in vain in the main building at Rikers, leaves without Nelson's having seen his children. He had been moved from one building to another, and they didn't find him. Nelson weeps. "Wednesday I'm going to be sentenced, and then I'll go upstate. That'll be the end of ever seeing them." The tears of that big, strong man are as grotesque as a death grimace. He is a mortally wounded lion.

José's family lives in the Bronx. There are three children. They came from Ecuador and have very little money. They live in a basement. It is too small, but it is close to the boiler room. The noise is unbearable. José is at Rikers.

This was an "express" marriage. I had just scratched my friend Fred from the list for the Thursday Bible circle. He had been very faithful during the year he was hcre and had been one of the lectors at Mass. He was prayerful and asked a lot of questions; he loved the Word and read and reflected on it intelligently and with interest.

He is just leaving for downstate to continue his sentence, which is fifteen years to life. I am not sure why he is here. In principle, I don't ask, unless, of course, someone talks to me about it. But his departure is a mistake. This very day he was supposed to get married, to give a regular civil form to his situation and that of his companion of many years. She is badly handicapped due to multiple sclerosis. They have a son who is hearing and speech impaired.

Well, I see him just as he is about to board the bus with barred windows to go to his new destination. "Father, could you tell the social workers? My wife should be in the visitors' room with the two witnesses, waiting for me. Tell them to hurry up." I run to Social Services, telephone right and left. They call Fred back. His wife, Ann, and the two witnesses are brought. The clerk is there. The ritual questions are posed, the papers signed, everything is in order. Done. The bus driver comes to see if we have finished. In less than five minutes Fred is married and put back on the bus, his wrists in handcuffs. Everything is done according to rule, everybody is kept in line. It is eleven o'clock. Ann has been at the prison since eight o'clock this morning. The two witnesses weep. I stand there in the background, wordless, empty even of thoughts. A marriage, a parting—a day in the life of the poor.

"When I was twelve years old my buddies and I stole something in a hardware store—oh, nothing big. It was petty larceny. At home my big brother took me aside and said to me: 'I promise not to do anything to you if you tell me the truth.' So I told him all the details of what had happened. After my confession I got the greatest beating of my life. I was so beat up that I swore I'd never tell the truth again."

Dave has just been arrested. It is the first time. The shock is more than he can bear. He weeps, cries, trembles, is totally agitated. Dave can't get over the fact that he is here. I see him often. He knows what is hurting him. With time, with the passing months, Dave changes. He soaks up the colors, the monotony of the prison. I see him become indifferent, cynical, avoiding contact, laughing at silly things, playing games. In five months Dave has become a different person. Dave is institutionalized.

I could go on this way forever, and so could a great many C.O.s and prisoners who know Rikers. Every day has its share of incidents. These stories of individuals represent my greatest frustrations here: the banality, the excess, the gross emptiness of certain situations, of certain places, the evidence of the deprivation of choices in this "castle of the poor," as they call the prison. Sometimes I long to be far away, to run out into the world of nature, to see big trees, to get away. I want to cling to faithful friendship, to everything that is solid, that lasts. I want to gorge myself on silence, on simple communion with what is complete, entire, whole. I want to walk the ways that are open to me, to leave the darkness behind.

The necessary conclusion is that Rikers Island is the quite natural result of situations that, humanly speaking, have no solution. I cannot embark here on the cold facts of the sociology of misery, passively dissecting the elements that lead to the abyss, plunging into the pitiless dryness of statistics. As a human being and a priest I can't help but be disturbed, enduring in my turn these thorns that attack and pierce the heart of a society that is existentially sick. What is certain, and what I did not know at the beginning is that to begin to see and to say that there are people who are suffering is to step into fetters that will last a lifetime.

6

OUR PARISH
BEHIND BARS

*Christianity is the story of beggars who tell other
beggars where to find bread.*

— Source unknown

I have known it for a long time. I have seen it for a long time. In other places I didn't think much about it. I gave it only limited attention. It was a minor detail. Now this almost makes me want to laugh.

There are a lot of keys at Rikers. There is nothing surprising about that. Here, there is plenty of use for keys!

In every building the control room is the brain and the eyes of the prison. The warning lights, the telephones, the buttons, the TV screens — everything that goes on in the blocks and corridors winds up or is reflected here.

Surrounded by very thick windows, proof against anything, here is the impregnable center that sees everything, commands everything, the real frontier between "inside" Rikers and "outside." So all the keys of the prison are stored here. Positioned and tagged on huge panels, they are passed to those who have the right to use them through a kind of revolving box embedded in the wall. The delivery, of course, is closely controlled. The person who asks for a key, the place, everything is identified, placed on file. Security, good order and efficiency demand it.

Thus every door, in order to be activated electrically, has its lock and key. These keys are usually very large, unique, certainly impossible to find in a lock shop. They are noisy; they invade your thoughts. Sometimes they hang in clusters from a C.O.'s belt. The keys are the most widespread, the most evident, the most haunting image before one's eyes when one is in prison.

But I am heading toward the HDM building and to the chapel inside it. I love that chapel, because little by little it has become for me, because of all that I have seen and experienced there, one of the sacred places in New York.

Above the altar there is an ordinary tabernacle, like those everywhere. At each Mass I put the ciborium with the reserved eucharistic species in it. Here is the saving presence offered to us, the radiant point, the impulse and the ferment, the leaven, before which every prayer can come to rest, every burden be laid down, every misery be accepted. Here is the bread of life.

But what I love about the tabernacle in the chapel of the HDM at Rikers, in this place that is so full of barriers, of contrived obstacles that challenge and defy solution, is that the door which shelters the ciborium, that very visible door, has nothing to hold it shut.

The only door in the whole building that has no key is here, at the center. And not even the most punctilious people here take exception to it. "My ways are not your ways."

Taking our starting point from this place of blazing life, which is the Body of Christ "given up for us," I now need to describe that which gathers around him, that which finds its life and direction from him within these walls. I need to describe the physical surroundings and the human beings who find in and through him their strength and direction, here, in prison. I must expand this heart of the church and offer it to all those who search for it and form it. The people, the places and the things here are witnesses of the church, its poverty, and its richness, its suffering and its glory. Our church is a church of sinners. Our church is a church of saints.

Someone has written, I cannot remember where, that before we can say yes to one world, we have to be able to say no to another. Before saying yes what is good, we have to say no to what is not good, to what is absurd, to this fragmented and drifting world that is so much with us.

Among the many different sense impressions that a person at Rikers can have I would like to share something that is given to us normally and simply. I will tell of those places and things, the human reality, the core of what has become, little by little, *our* parish behind bars. I emphasize the word *our* because there is so much that is implied in it.

At Rikers there is, practically speaking, only one institution with a special and defined place for each religious group: the HDM. In the other buildings, C 95 for example, all the confessions and denominations have to take turns using the same room, one service following another. That places a severe limit on the sense of taking solid possession of a sacred space for a community of believers. No doubt every chaplin here would have a lot to say about that imposed cheapening of meaning, that blurring of distinctions, the necessity to begin from nothing each time and to carry everything with us.

As everywhere in the Christian world, the chapel is the privileged place of assembly, the place where the Lord is present. Here is our first obligation, if we are sent here for the sake of a community, a church. This is true for these spiritual reasons and also, frankly, for simple reasons of health. In a world of bars and of unhappiness, there is nothing more depressing than not to have one simple place, one corner of beauty where an experience can be transformed or celebrated. There is nothing more deadly than not to have any chance to share in depth and rhythm, thus reaffirming the humanity of our lives. That depression, that death is the daily, brutal manna of the prison, the no I spoke of above, to which we in turn have to say no. So this house of God, this worshipful place at the very center of Rikers, is the anti-prison, the refuge, the sanctuary, the House of the People, where human laws can suddenly become very fragile and superficial, where they can even dissolve, where, finally, everything happens because we are all awaited and desired.

FREE ME LORD

In the choir of the chapel this sharp, naive painting of the head of a prisoner between two fists painfully clutching thick bars, with two tears rolling down his hollow cheeks, grabs the attention of visitors as soon as they walk in. The portrait was done by a well-known inmate of Rikers, Baptista, a passionate and talented painter. Baptista was one of the main restorers of this chapel. At the back, on a series of large panels, he painted a skilled and splendid reproduction of the creation of the human being in the Sistine Chapel. On another wall he did another large copy of the expressive head of Christ by Rembrandt. Many people, both visitors and prisoners, who come here for the first time, ask questions about Baptista. Such gifts are noticed, even at Rikers.

Paintings, carpet, an altar bearing an eighteenth century crucifix found in a church and restored by the prisoners; all these are joined by a single statue. This sober, peaceful image of the Virgin of the Poor from Banneux, Belgium, was sent as a special gift expressing the solidarity of distant friends. There is a set of stations of the cross in carved wood. The floor is impeccably waxed, and the green plants never lack for volunteers to care for and water them. "The chapel is a place that's lived-in," says Ed, a Puerto Rican prisoner. He adds: "I have just two peaceful times in this prison: when I am asleep and when I come here. I know some people who would come here a lot oftener if they could."

Like everything else in the prison, any meeting here, any celebration is subject to controls. Freedom of religion is guaranteed everywhere, but it remains subject to conditions; inspections are more or less discreet, depending on the individuals in charge, or even the day's happenings. A disturbance, somebody missing from the island for example, calls for extra "counts," even in the middle of Mass.

The Mass is the heart, center, source and end of everything we are seeking here. It is a very emotional time, a time of festival and community. Certainly it can be one of the week's rare moments of relaxation and reunion among the prisoners. But it is here, in a unique and essential manner, that a sorrow, a belief, a hope surviving among the prisoners who are believers can find its expression. These people come from everywhere, although quite often a majority are Latin Americans. Many of them wear medals or a rosary around their necks. Sometimes they stand for a long time in front of the altar, before the crucifix. They sing, in English or Spanish:

> There will be peace in the valley for me.
> There will be no sadness, no sorrow.
> No trouble I'll see.
> There will be peace in the valley for me.

Today we hear the gospel of the healing of the paralytic in Matthew. "Your sins are forgiven." Some stand up spontaneously to join their personal intentions to the prayer of the faithful. They pray "for all those like us all over the world who live under oppression." There are symbolic gestures, long handclasps during the exchange of peace, communion under both species. They beat their breasts: *Te pedimos perdon, Senōr.* The final hymn speaks of affliction and hope:

Lord, I'm tired, I'm so weak,
Lord, I'm alone,
Through the storm, through the night,
Lead me home to the light,
Take my hand, O Lord,
Lead me home, lead me home.

The Mass is ended. There is the final blessing, the last greeting exchanged between friends, then the whole group tidies the chapel and the altar, arranges the books, and so on. Slowly they leave to return to the blocks, shaking hands, exchanging thanks weighty with friendship and longing.

EUCHARIST

How do I live the eucharist? How do I celebrate the eucharist? Times have changed since I was ordained in 1961, and modes of expression have also changed. But it is still the Mass, the Pascha, the Christ. Now, during the week, I celebrate alone or, more often, with my sisters and brothers.

Most of the time I celebrate in a little chapel set aside within an apartment in Brooklyn, in the easy intimacy of friendship. It is a simple sharing, usually in the evening, surrounded by the more or less intrusive buzz of the street or the neighbors.

The prayer is quite naturally carried forward by the group, in free expression and singing adapted to the occasion, after the gospel or during the intentions. People do what they want to.

This "half hour of truth" is the lighthouse or reference point of every day, as necessary as the daily bread.

Whether we kneel or sit on the floor, the sacred space is there. Each of us occupies it. It is the privileged and inexhaustible moment of faith, like every gathering drawn together for the Pasch.

Though every Mass has its identical weight of richness and gift, independent of the place in which it is celebrated, and though the Body of Christ is made to be realized everywhere, the one I celebrate on Sundays takes place in a prison. There, Mass takes up the whole morning. I celebrate three times in three different places.

I would say that Sunday is my most difficult day, the one that exhausts me the most. There is no comparison with my normal weekly work and the individual encounters in the prison.

Since the purpose is to celebrate with prisoners, all of whom are wounded or scarred people, I have an absolute need to prepare ahead of time. I find time for it during the week. I meet with a Jesuit friend, who is a kind of beggar for God in the New York street world, and a sister who also works at the prison. Together we take up the Mass texts and "chew" them thoroughly. We seek to be schooled by the gospel; we are certain that we are in touch with Life, that there is an urgency, something to be done, to be said. This meeting is always very authentic. There is a common will to be present "in spirit and in truth," as disciples.

I am not saying that we achieve this, that we are always conscious of it, but there is at least evidence that what we are doing is dangerous, demanding and entirely fascinating.

Scripture itself is nourishment, fire, medicine and mirror for us. We seek to take God at God's word, we listen, we let ourselves be captivated. For example, we realize together that we need add nothing to the words of Jesus, that we simply have to listen to them, that only the Father in heaven is good, that everything outside the truth is a prison.

In short, I need this atmosphere, this kind of prayer that is willed, called forth, discovered, that compromises us, in order to be able to accept quietly whatever comes, without a superficial respect for what is on the surface, without having to assume a role from the outset. It amounts to a kind of effacement of function.

All this is necessary because on Sunday morning I have to deal with people who are broken and lying at the bottom of a well, naked, their backs to the wall. The eucharist, death and resurrection, the depths of the Good News can do nothing but offer the greatest acceptance possible to all these cries.

On the one hand, what we have here is a base community, often very far from having a classical ecclesial form, but with its own sort of motivation: a community that sings, prays and listens.

On the other hand, it is a sacrament, new every time. That means that I need to modify and discard some things that would be normal in other places. For example, I have to avoid a too-careful fidelity to rubrics and an excessive sensitivity to good order. This does not mean that I bring everything down to the level of those whose attention is veiled or distracted, or who are preoccupied with something else, but that the liturgy, in all its vitality and mystery, is not there to help us to live, to support and console us, but to change us.

We are not there to solve all the world's problems, including our own. Our coming together is, every time, an apprenticeship for each of us; we allow our lives, and the life of the world, to be scraped and rubbed by a gift, by a peace that is not from here, by a truth that has "endured all things" (1 Cor 13:7).

The transparency of Christ will or will not find its way. Ours are the place, the time, the various means that are brief, limited, transient, hurried; his are the depth of presence, the grace that revivifies.

> This is the church's patrimony,
> the communion of saints,
> the "today" of God.
> Make the leap and catch fire.
> "Great is the mystery of our faith."

MONASTIC CELLS

Who would have thought that a prison could be a house of prayer? If "porno cells" hung with *Playboy* photos offering their fantasies to the prisoners are not absent from Rikers, there are still others that resemble the cells of monks, thickly hung with rosaries, pious images or carefully framed photos of loved ones. "You're at the bottom of the well here," says Alvaro. "The suffering is greater, but you feel yourself closer to God." Another says: "You can always adapt, hold on physically. But spiritually, you need help. Without our Christian community at Rikers, I couldn't make it."

A real church has been built up behind the bars, composed of those who come to Mass, wanting to pray or to learn how to pray, joining the Bible classes and the retreats that are held three times a year. In face of an institutional logic that seeks to break people, or at least the rapport between them, this Christian community rows against the current and sometimes seems to be the only lifeboat. Alvaro again: "Without faith you live like an animal. Through the faith and hope in a better life that we are searching for together, I find a peace and calm that help me to go on."

It has been established, proved, experienced, guaranteed from the beginning of the ages: prayer strengthens. If I try to plumb the depths of what we might call the religious experience in prison, the word that constantly recurs is *prayer*. It is like a cork; it cannot be kept submerged. As necessary, as daily, as natural as air for a bird, it supports life and gives it wings. It puts things in perspective, like the view from a mountaintop in clear weather. "Who shall live on your holy mountain?" asks the psalm. That saying about the mountain has a lot of resonance for me: leaving while it is still completely dark, at one or two o'clock in the morning, walking in silence, in single file, going upward, sometimes slowly, sometimes rapidly, sometimes at places that are extremely challenging and exposed, and each time finding a new world at daybreak. I still carry in my head too many very precise images of the place, the harmony, the beginnings, too many memories of blessed moments that reconcile the individual with the all. It is enough to listen and look in order to participate by a kind of osmosis in the solidity, endurance and transparency of a new world. You can call it ordinary contemplation if you will, but it is a contemplation full of treasures, the kind that sometimes arise between those who join in the walk together. They are without masks. To struggle together, depending on one another in the risk and the effort, is like giving blood, giving being to each other. I have never appreciated the word *group* so much as on those climbs.

But all that is only a comparison. And, like every comparison, it is deficient. For if we have to pray, in the sense of the saying "with all your heart, with all your soul, with all your strength," it is also true that we have to receive everything. "Behold, I stand at the door and knock. If anyone opens to me I will enter." Prayer is like a gift that is always offered in every human life. It is entirely the work of the human person; it is entirely the gift of God. Prayer is there every day to put an end to that cancerous idea that God is absent.

THE POWERS OF EVIL

It is as impossible to achieve silence in the midst of noise—and God knows there are a few decibels on Rikers Island, close by LaGuardia Airport—as it would be to maintain zones of pure water in a polluted river. Then how can a spiritual life be possible here, how can anyone flee from and deny the environment that frames every life and is written in red ink here—the environment of evil, of sin? I believe—and my belief is supported by quite a few years of experience—that being in Rikers means getting in touch with what can be described as the forces of evil. Undoubtedly, in the life of everyone who struggles in the Lord, that encounter will come, one day or another. It is an encounter that becomes a confrontation for each one of us. The forces of evil are the obstacles that bar the road to communion with God. The simple, little sin I accept in myself opens me to their influence. And there is no one spot that is more vulnerable than any other. Anyone can say yes or no at any point. Everything depends on what kind of "doorkeeper" I am, on my acceptance or refusal.

On the other hand, it is difficult to speak of a devil or demon. There is nothing more disorienting to any subject than a chronic restlessness, such as one sees everywhere here. As we learn, and as we know, reason and the law of the gospel are sufficient for our judgment and conduct. And there is often a lot of good sense in skepticism. Excess, even and especially when we are speaking of the devil, is only a mirage, an insignificant remnant. And yet, as we believe, the devil, too, is only a creature.

Still, without being nervously on the lookout for traces of him—which would put us quite on the wrong track—I firmly believe that what we experience and see here is not foreign to what I am obliged to call his presence, not only in the many traces of deviations or perversions, or the fact of hatred cultivated, carefully considered and expressed, but even more in the "opacity" that has seeped into every part of the prison. I believe that the Evil One, the Adversary, the Accuser, the Spirit of Discord, finds a prime locus in what goes on here. Hate and rancor undoubtedly open the door for him. The many situations of violence, noise, sick nerves, unbearable isolation, aberrant ways of life and of intelligent malice that seem to bury forever the simple right to a life that, if not normal, is at least livable, are like hammers driving in the nail of skepticism about God. In any case they swiftly massacre the most precious of God's gifts; they change a human being into something inhuman. (I am not speaking primarily of structures now, or of the aberrations of a specific system. What I have in mind is more the evil that exists in heads and hearts, not what is bad in external things, even though it is often apparent that there is a connection between the two.)

We have bird sanctuaries in the country; why not people sanctuaries everywhere? They could be as much tied to whatever retribution is possible and to compassion for the victims as "sustenance for the souls" of the guilty. Everything that is brutal here, everything that is not healed and is, in fact, self-aggravating, all this emptiness is dead. I doubt whether getting accustomed to the darkness can attenuate its effects. But if a plant deprived of water and sun will quickly wither and fade, how can we fail to understand, how can we be surprised when, in an air that is so polluted, something ultimately breaks? "Life is so difficult around here, you know!"

The prison is an existentially sick society. I don't want to paint everything black, despite the fact that there is a superabundance of material for that endeavor here. I am simply trying to get at what I cannot pass over in silence in this place. To what or to whom am I to attribute all of this, if not to what St. Paul calls "the powers of this world of darkness"? The Fathers of the church tell us that there is in the world a body of sin controlled by the devil, opposed to the body of the church controlled by Christ. But it is not for us to decide in all cases and at all times where the boundary lies and where the divisions are (although it is quite true that there are objective and essential norms for conscience and morality, and that we are not permitted to play with the truth). I sympathize with the painter Rouault, who could not understand judges. The necessity of judging on the basis of evidence and of relying on nothing else does not deny the limits of what I know about my brother, about his heart. What I see is very probably different from and not to be compared with what God knows. And only God can separate the inextricable ingredients of good and evil, everything that is part of our world today. But that will come at the end, even if in the mean time everyone who believes in Jesus is called to bear fruit, to devote his or her strength to the reign of God that is present and to come.

At Rikers, just as everywhere else, we cannot preach the gospel to the devil. But for our little parish, as for a very large one, there are preliminary recognitions, premonitions that are already certainties about the result of the contest.

Moving through the weeds in the prison, in spite of the nausea it brings, is to seek the arms of God while learning again and again the prudence of the serpent and the simplicity of the dove. It means not letting go for an instant of what came forth at the Easter dawn as a victorious and final gift. It means knowing and learning again and again that the only real results, beyond apparent success or failure, come about through that means alone.

My friend Mary understands this so well that, though she is physically handicapped and ordinarily not at all inclined to such gestures, she sometimes goes to spend a moment in church to pray for the world of Rikers. This link in the chain of faith joins her to those others, in their very different place and circumstances; it gives life and tone to the whole group. We are all patients in the recovery room. And there is only one place to look to for the best treatment, only one method of care. We find them in and with a group, a community, a God!

THE BREVIARY OF THE POOR

But how can we distinguish the expression of a simple and sincere faith from some kind of vague and omnipresent religiosity in prison? Religion is very much in demand here. It has set up shop in a good location. It has public recognition. Pious pictures are framed in gold or silver paper. Among the profane tattoos there are little crosses, and medals hang on chains over the T-shirts. Thousands of rosaries have been distributed and are still being given out. They come from everywhere: from nursing homes, from the sick, from concerned friends, from people unknown and far away.

Why are there so many rosaries here? Perhaps it is a way for the prisoners to recover the image of their mothers, their wives or even their girlfriends. The rosary, like the medals, little crosses and pictures, all the business of religious knickknacks that, in other places, would seem rather undigested and forced, is for them, here in this gigantic, anonymous prison, a sign of recognition and of ownership, and a means of affirmation.

The rosary is the breviary of the poor. Its simplicity, its profundity, its tradition are rooted in faith that the holy Virgin will help us find and live with Jesus; it is a powerful aid to breathing in here. How many times have I been surprised by that truth in this or that person! Of course it is often necessary to explain, to make distinctions, to correct and to purify their belief, to help them get away from magic and empty gestures. Some say: "If I weren't here, I wouldn't pray." Or they say: "Being in prison is what has forced me to pray." Why start off by rejecting such a point of departure? Why be too quick to doubt the sincerity of a movement of faith? Our births are all hidden. Starting out on the road is already a big thing. A lot of those here ask for times for adoration, for periods of silence. Collective silence in the presence of God has a completely different dimension than the "normal" silence each prisoner must deal with in his cell. I have participated many times in a very powerful experience of prayer. In the middle of the silence or the terrible noise in this prison a collective silence is the most beautiful kind of prayer. It brings to mind the peace of which Isaiah speaks (Is 11:6-9).

THE SCHOOL OF FAITH

Besides the Mass, individual or community prayer and study courses on the Bible play a major role in the structuring of this prison parish. As with every other religious activity, a selection is quickly made between those who are looking for a momentary diversion—they give up quickly—and those who come seeking an opportunity for catechesis. I prefer to offer something solid in these classes. I cannot permit myself any kind of detached, academic study, much less lofty sessions and carefully elaborated lessons. But it is easy to choose between the peripheral and the essential: the gospels, especially Matthew and John, the beatitudes, the Our Father, the book of Job, the psalms, and so on. As in climbing a steep mountain, it is necessary to proceed cautiously and to have a guide. It takes effort on the part of all, and at the same time, we need to let the Holy Spirit show the way. We are learning together, because we are hungry together. We have to create the atmosphere; the more relaxed and naturally appealing it is, the richer the dialogue will be. Sometimes a simple moment of truth is enough to compensate for all the obstacles and problems of the day, the ever-present contingencies of the prison.

MAKING A RETREAT

The retreats are the most powerful times for our Christian community. Together with Sister Simone and the other sisters in her house, we are very attached to these retreats, for each is special, a very moving time, preceded by preparations that are more and more absorbing as the day gets closer. The magnitude of the retreats, the investment of all kinds of energy they demand, require that we cannot allow ourselves this "adventure" more than about once every three months. This rhythm is our maximum. I have no hesitation in placing a high value on these moments, these days of transformation, even when we are doing them for the thirtieth time. Within the whole official system, which legally and by definition is dry, rigid, gray and cold — but not at all opposed, since it accepts this quite willingly — these are the notes of color and grace breaking through all systems and conventions, the breath of air for everyone, the collective discovery of something better and something more.

This retreat is religious; it takes place in a group; and it happens in a prison. These three related elements indicate the reason why we cling so strongly to it. A church behind bars, an approach to the gospel that is not merely individual but communal, an interior refusal of degradation like a sudden outbreak of one's whole being, undertaking a journey with others — all this attracts us. If I dared, I would say that we have all that is needed to form a "gang." For here, as everywhere, the individual is in trouble. Groups form very quickly on all sides, one against the others, often stereotyped, seeking extreme expressions. Groups set the tone, "make the law," with customary rules, sanctions, peer pressure — a subterranean world completely outside official conventions and forms of justice, born of confinement and proximity.These groups achieve more than survival. Within the given limits, they have the power they seize for themselves. So, in prison, a gang of Christians coming out of their cages has a weight that I am sure very few, on the outside, would recognize. There is a light here that has nothing to do with any rule or regulation of a human system.

Our Bible circles are shaped by the inner circle, the base group, and by patient preparation. Only those prisoners who are willing to put themselves at risk, week after week, to be involved, to wait in the church to see who will be placed on the list for the retreat, are here. That is why these retreats are always a gathering, a place of charged and privileged encounter. That is also the reason why we say no to many others — and there are always some who would simply like to spend the day, with completely different motivation.

Need I say that we are very wide awake at such times? For in prison, too, one has those strange temptations to "do good," that is, to get lost in the psychology of compassion. We do not envision anything like perfection or elitism. Jesus has come, all too clearly, for the children, the broken and the lost. But because all of this requires a choice, a certain shape and form, without any prejudgment of the variety of landscapes and situations in which the gifts of heaven are bestowed, and also without seeing ourselves as the appointed dispensers of those gifts, we have learned not to accept any participants for this very different journey other than those who have chosen this way.

The retreats are usually held in the institution's visiting room, since the inmates are allowed to have up to three members of their family with them. We saw very quickly how beneficial it could be for isolated men, not simply to meet one another in a family context, but also to accompany one another, with their families, into a shared spiritual life. Here, for example, is Bernie, seated between his father and mother, whose marriage broke up a long time ago, and who have found each other again in the company of their son, reconciled and happy.

The success of the retreats depends on their preparation: a questionnaire on the chosen theme is given out in advance to each participant. At seven A.M. the invited guests from outside are waiting at the entrance to the bridge to Rikers. They are taken by a special bus to the room where the retreat will be held. Volunteers and religious sisters keep the children busy writing, drawing and playing. We take the midday meal together. There are snacks and desserts; Mass is celebrated. Everything in our heads is very far removed from the prison. Or, to put it another way, this is a day when everything is different.

But let me illustrate by an example:

On this particular morning, counting the volunteers, the prisoners — all dressed in very clean, dark blue dungarees — and some of their families, we are exactly 204 persons gathered in the visiting room of the prison. The room is none too large, or rather, this number of people completely fills it. We have decorated the room with beautiful posters and bright colors. On one side is a buffet with coffee, pastry, and soda. The chairs are arranged in a semicircle. There is a microphone at the center.

All of this is already completely out of the ordinary and helps to establish the ambience, to change the atmosphere. Little details weigh heavily here, far from the ponderous bars and gates. Of course, there are C.O.s here, too. But they also enter into the ambience or respect it; they keep discreetly quiet throughout the day.

There is Juan, a new deacon and a longtime volunteer, so capable and so valuable with his guitar. He helps organize things and leads the singing, for these days are never without songs and chants of praise.

There, too, is Bernadette, a Franciscan sister who, after we have greeted each one, takes a few minutes to introduce the day's program. The chosen theme is forgiveness. Bernadette concludes by posing three questions to be discussed in small groups:

1) Is it impossible to forgive others if one has not already been pardoned oneself?

2) Have you had the experience of not being forgiven by others? If so, what did that do to you?

3) Have you had the experience of having forgiveness refused — of wanting to forgive someone, but your pardon not being accepted? How did you react to that?

We divide into about a dozen groups, spread around the room, where we reflect on these questions, communicating in

English and Spanish. We need bilingual volunteers, since many of the Hispanics do not speak any English. I will simply note some of the reactions among those I have heard. In their dryness, they are the product, the precious earth around which the dialogue turns.

"Maybe God forgives, but society doesn't."

"How can you forgive when all you get are blows? In prison it's a sign of weakness to forgive, or to do anything good. It's more acceptable to show your teeth, to make people afraid."

A sister says: "Peace follows forgiving. You feel completely different." "But sister, you don't live in a cell the way we do. You can't know what it's like!"

"I asked in front of witnesses to be able to confess in the presence of my wife. That way, my wife saw that my repentance was serious, because I wanted it to be public."

"Not forgiving yourself is being like Judas. It kills you!"

"I can forgive myself, but my family doesn't want to hear anything about forgiving me."

"It may be easy to forgive, but it sure is hard to forget."

Each group has a chance to speak, each one choosing its own style and respecting pace, rhythm and even silence as a means of expression. We are so unaccustomed to these things here! But little by little, gently, quietly, something is born within the room. One by one, starting from the point of view where they find themselves, the participants find that they are led toward a quality that I think is preserved only in children: the ability to enter into a mystery, to see beyond the immediate. "I had to come to prison to see that," one of them says. "This is the first time I have felt safe here," says another.

Normally we bring together the results of all the group discussions. They are summarized and reflected on by all those present. But this time a visit from the warden, the head of the prison, does not allow for it. They will have to wait until later, because he has chosen to spend some time with us, to tell us how much he appreciates what is happening here within his institution on this retreat day. He even hopes that there will be more of them, and wants to help bring it about, because he sees that what is touched on here will enter deeply into many lives. There is a dialogue, conducted in terms of respect and dignity;

there is applause. "At least, on a day like this, you feel like a normal human being." "Just imagine, you can even begin to look at the warden as a friend!" These are echoes of powerful moments that will leave their mark. And the children, singing "We Are the World" at the tops of their voices and beautifully off key before an audience that is totally absorbed and attentive, express the beauty of communion and of a world that has been recaptured. There will be a meal taken in freedom, a reunion. At Mass there will be singing, silence, reflection. There are smiles, tears and a certainty that is completely new and unhoped for, that remains to comfort us as we depart. For the hour of parting comes all too quickly. The prisoners leave first, in one direction, and then the volunteers and the families, in the other direction.

But in the evening after all that, as on every occasion after this kind of gathering, something extra remains: a community of brothers and sisters completely "bowled over" at being seen and recognized.

The wounds are not gone; they are still there, open, very painful. But they have had today; they have called forth a discovery and nurtured a step forward. Each one, with all the best that is in him or her, in a thousand forms, has bestowed on others a treasure without price, because each one has once more experienced an abundance of openness, a surplus of life. We have become too rich not to believe in anything but ridicule, failure or fear.

THE PEOPLE ON THE "GOOD" SIDE OF THE BARS: A DIALOGUE WITH A D.W. (DEPUTY WARDEN)

"Inside myself I have a lot of sympathy for the inmates. I see what a loss of freedom means, what they have to go through. But on the outside, in my work, I have to go by the book. My margin for choice is not very big. There is a lot of pressure here.

"In my work, three things are necessary. I call them 'the three P's.' (1) Paper, because you have to put everything down on paper; you have to make reports. (2) Patience, because the obstacles here are multiplied, compared with free society. Life here is slowed down, and the prison is huge. (3) Prayer, to keep my sanity. Without it, you can't survive."

This D.W. is a friend of mine. He has had years of experience at Rikers and doesn't mind stopping to talk. He knows what is going on and lets the chips fall where they may, even on the C.O.s. I agree fully with him about his "three P's." But in applying the word *patience* to the prisoners also, without forgetting their victims, I remember that "time is all we have here, it's all that's left to us." There is another difference. It regards the word *paper*, with respect to the chaplains' ministry. It is the conviction that spiritual things cannot easily be reported, especially not on official forms. Between a paper and a reality, there is all the difference between life and death. The gifts of God cannot be measured in terms of human success. We need completely different criteria to discern them.

In short, for myself, and without any condescending, I might say that I know a little bit about the world of the employees of the Department of Corrections (DOC), and I can readily witness, like all of them, to the tense moments, the emptiness, and often the enormous responsibility that are their lot here. Having said that, I have no desire to enter into general controversies or to make those easy criticisms that are in vogue. I see the DOC as the pure and simple product of our present society with its diversity, its failures, its heroism, its moods and its tedium: it is the responsibility of us all. This is not meant to invite passivity or lack of interest. Moreover, enforcing law and order can never be limited to a mechanical abstraction, a matter of anticipated and completely codified actions. There is always the human factor, the thousand and one imponderables, fecund with richness or with internal disaster, with fidelity or abandonment. I understand the division that my friend, the D.W., experiences. For him, it does not extend to the point of "tolerating the intolerable"; it rejects evil. It starts from the Calvary of reality and seeks after Life.

"When I leave the prison," says a C.O., "I don't take it home with me. I try to forget it. I don't talk about it any more after I leave the gate. I don't want the prison to have an effect on my children." Certainly, but balance is not effected simply through silence, a forcible burying of the irrational that can so easily surface in the prison. It needs an outlet. The C.O. who shouts at a frightened group in a corridor, "When I meet a human being, I treat him like a human being. When I meet an animal, I treat it like an animal," has already passed beyond a certain point at which he, too, has become a victim. The higher part of him is suffering. He no longer realizes that he is drowning himself in the prison. What he is doing is destroying him.

Another says to me: "When you get involved with too many needs of insignificant people, you make monsters of them." He, too, has a hemorrhage of humanity within himself, if by "too many needs" he means to imply the refusal of simple human recognition. Punishing evil with evil has, on this earth, opened the door to a great many catastrophes. Fidelity and certitude, which by necessity are simple therapies of protection and encouragement, should not simply be identified in advance, but nourished and made vigorous. It is a matter of the dignity of each person, of the universal value in everyone, and for a Christian, it is a matter of seeing the face of Christ everywhere.

I have already said that at Rikers every building has its personality, its own character. There is nothing remarkable about that, since every institution is totally autonomous, within the limits of the common rules applicable to all. Thus it is the people, from the warden down to the last employee and even the prisoners, who make all the difference in producing a home spirit, made up of the contributions and deficiencies of all. It is a very sensitive terrain where reputation, atmosphere and a way of doing things are created, a terrain that is often very demanding—physically, psychologically, spiritually—with all kinds of victims. (A chaplain has said, "To work in a prison, you need an infinite capacity for disappointment.") But you also discover a family at all levels of this world and its hierarchy. You find people who are extremely rich in their hearts and their way of looking at things, in their humanity and way of being. Some of them have not received promotion, have not sought it and do not want it, and are respected by everyone just as they are. They have experience and wisdom. They are the pillars of the place.

As a chaplain I have a certain number of activities that are normally expected and carried out as part of the job, but from time to time I also enter into a strong and effective cooperation with the authorities. How many times have I, together with Sister Simone and others, received an invitation phrased in a variety of ways: "We are interested in what you are trying to do. Proceed as seems best to you. You are in a tight spot, but it's your ball game." Without over-confidence, we welcome their trust and take it as something very serious and pregnant with consequences. To hear someone say to you, with a gracious openness, "Be the church you want to be with the people who are here," certainly triggers a good deal of far reaching reflection, leading up to this simple and difficult and inevitable point: This Christ you talk about, the one who wants to be behind these bars — well, you are responsible for him. Show them what he's worth. They will take you at your word." As if the world all around us spoke with the voice of God.

Let me conclude this point with the words of a prisoner that I have made my own: "When I get out, I want to send a lot of thank you cards to the people from all over that I have met here at Rikers. I never said a word about it, but many times I have received a lot from them. They taught me a lot."

7

STRESS

Let me see things as they are, and don't let anything throw dust in my eyes.

— Thérèse of Lisieux

I return from a week's absence from Rikers. I visited family and friends. It was sunshine and moments of happiness. Today is my first morning walking down the corridors of the jail. Suddenly, there is violence. Four inmates are fighting in Block 4. Help comes too late. The four prisoners are wounded, one critically. There is blood on the floor and on the wall. I didn't see what happened exactly; I see only the terrible results. If I had forgotten violence during my week's break, once again I am confronted with the folly of this world of isolation and emptiness.

After this incident I begin my regular visits to the prisoners. There is the ex-policeman who wanted to make a little extra money and who now finds himself in prison. His professional life, his family, have all been devastated. We speak, but I listen for the most part. He begs me to pray for him; he asks me to come and see him again.

The next inmate I visit speaks of the stupidity of his brother who is prison upstate. This stupidity on his brother's part was his taking vengeance on an "enemy," whom he paralyzed for life. I can't remember the reason he gave for the crime; all I remember is that his brother prepared the revenge for two years. All those years with only one idea in his head: to do harm. One result, among others, is that now he has six years in prison to "enjoy" his victory.

One visit like this after another—this will be my day at Rikers. My vacation is very far away now as I am re-immersed in the maelstrom of the prison. There is nothing especially unique or exceptional in these events, which are part of our world today. There is only the closeness of this daily darkness. On the level of simple psychology, whether one is a prisoner or not, the world of the prison is a world of stress. It is impossible for anyone to maintain a clinical detachment here. To systematically refuse to show any trace of emotion in the name of a supposed professionalism or in the name of preserving one's mental health at any price impoverishes any kind of communication or human presence. There are stress management programs to assist with the work. I'd like to describe one of my experiences.

I attend a day's program on stress with the chaplains of the New York Department of Corrections. There are thirty-five of us, including rabbis, imams, male and female Protestant ministers, Catholic sisters, brothers and priests. A sister from Ossining who is trained in psychology will conduct the session. We are in Queens, at Cathedral College in Douglaston, a spacious place with lovely trees, far from all the pressure and noise of the prison.

What I remember, beyond the information we were given and the tests to which we all submitted in order to evaluate our degree of stress, is the exercise on centering prayer as described by the sister and suggested to all of us, from whatever denomination. For twenty minutes, comfortably seated, eyes lowered, we created an emptiness in our spirits to be filled solely by a mantra, a word expressing a quality, a relationship to the God we adore. *Maranatha* was proposed for the Christians. I recognize the psychological fruit of this exercise, regaining control over the crazy thoughts in our heads, and the spiritual point, soaking up God as a sponge soaks up water, as lungs take in air, letting go of what burdens us, "erasing the tape" of frustrations, of what is poisonous. It is a major effort at housecleaning, in which things quietly return to their places, far removed from all the aggressivity and jostling that presses upon us. I acknowledge the good effects of this, the guarantee of success when it is a question of rediscovering one's center, roots, origins — simply of finding oneself. Indeed, here is a good method to use against rampant fatigue, against the threatening drain on energy and nerves, a method that easily puts one's head back on one's shoulders, recovers an elementary and precious equilibrium, something that is so necessary and that we miss so much when it fails us.

I can't help thinking at this point of the chaplain, always very active, visible, open and committed, who, after eight years in the prison, said to me: "I can't think any more. I have become a machine." So he was functioning out of instinct, on the spur of the moment. It became impossible for him. He had to leave. And his departure had every appearance of flight. I am not passing judgment on the responsibility for or the circumstances of this particular "burnout," but it is true that the means of survival in prison are anything but obvious, and are not to be acquired by oneself. As with an automobile, periodic servicing is necessary. You have to know how to disengage regularly in order to go on living, whether with a mantra or something else.

But I have often thought about that form of silent and cleansing prayer practiced by the chaplains with regard to my imprisoned friends. For if there is any group faced with fatigue, lack of energy and poor self-esteem, it is this one, these people who are here because someone has put them here. I am talking about the ones, whether criminals or not, who are seeking a way far removed from the confusion and tension and who come to me asking for such a way. So sometimes in our Bible circle we practice this exercise, this working silence. And it is always different from doing it alone. The quality of the group exerts pressure, creates reflections, has an impact on each of us. There are moments we all notice, that we all remember because this "loss of time" refills the world with space; it is simply gift and grace.

Nevertheless, I would like to add that the rich, beneficial, therapeutic "emptiness" of these precious moments cannot replace the massive heritage of tradition, especially for prisoners. I am thinking of those violent moments of crisis, the cries, the revived confidence we find, for example, in the psalms, the inexhaustible and manifold faces of the word of God in the Bible. As Andre Chouraki says: "In the psalms, even if the innocent person is often killed, still it is always the evil one who is vanquished." For people who are empty of everything, left in the desert, dying of hunger and thirst, how necessary it is to move them, to quicken and enliven their march with images, with events emerging from faith through all time! For that you need material, you need history, you need to study. You also have to grow in knowledge. Like all of us, the prisoners want to understand and to love. They look at Christ and see clearly that on the cross, with or without a mantra, he lived his offering to the Father.

That meeting of chaplains was a good one. Everyone agreed in saying that, in the midst of the depressing prison system, vigilance is absolutely necessary to avoid being trapped and destroyed before you know it. We all tell what we do, what means we choose to keep a cool head and catch our breath: music, games, physical exercise, and others. Certainly, all that is obvious and results from the fragility of the common human condition. I would simply point to another experience, the human and spiritual experience of a church, the necessity of a solid group and a fundamental vision. If we forget that, if we let our perspectives, plans, motivations slip and do not continue to nourish ourselves with them, then I think it is time to leave, to seek some other place in which to repair the damage. There are situations in which it would be more than simply "too bad" if we went the wrong way. There are joys too precious for us to persist in fleeing them or in resigning ourselves to not seeing them. Sister Simone tells me: "In prison I am not giving; I am receiving." Jean Vanier said, when he was in New York: "When you become gratuitous, free, all the world around you becomes free."

Saying no to the darkness, thinking positively, is undoubtedly the beginning for many, and particularly for chaplains. In contrast—I hope more than an apparent contrast—to many other elements in the penitentiary system, we chaplains have no small opportunity to achieve a possible coherence, a total and radical vision. We can live what we are doing. I am not saying that a C.O. who stands by a door and opens and shuts it a thousand times a day is necessarily excluded from being a whole person. From the C.O.'s point of view there are, no doubt, other approaches to be taken without abandoning one's responsibility. There are also necessary places of cooperation, of solidarity, of opportunities for social impact, for vigilance on behalf of justice when a group is present and willing to reflect and to act. . . . But to return to the subject of stress, whether one is a chaplain or not, an inmate, a C.O., I think the only way out is upward, where one can discover the personal meaning of the gospel's word, the word *transfigured*.

"What do you achieve with those prisoners?" a well-off and elderly woman once asked me in a challenging way.

"Only God knows for sure," I answered. "But for all the troubles and challenges I would not apply for any other work. It may appear strange, but the reality is that the prisoners teach me a great deal."

8

RELIGIOUS DIVISIONS

The terrible hour when God is not real and when
I go on loving him all the same.

— Marie Noel

T he prison, our parish . . . beyond eucharistic celebrations and catechesis in the framework of Scripture courses, we have baptisms, visits to the sick, to families, and so on. I will speak about these last in more detail a little later on. But we have no Catholic marriages here, because of the difficulty of making the canonical inquiries (on account of the separation of the inmates from their families) and the fragility of unions contracted when the walls of a prison separate the two partners.

It is often difficult to explain this decision to the men and women concerned, but I cannot help approving of it. For really, how can we sacramentally affirm a union in which one spouse lives inside the bars and the other outside? Before coming here some of these inmates already lived in quasi-marital partnerships. Why did they wait until they were in Rikers before asking and obtaining a religious blessing on their marriage? It is an action that involves the church too deeply for us to banalize it or weaken its fundamental vision. There remains the possibility of a legal, civil marriage, or even a religious ceremony if such is permitted by other denominations or confessions.

I cannot get involved at this point in all the implications of the question of marriage in prison. That would take us far beyond these pages. My purpose here is simply to allude to something that is often perceived as a source of scandal, and that is very difficult to accept, even here in prison — religious division.

The inmates experience this division from the beginning of their incarceration; some of them for the first time in their lives. They do not understand why the Catholics, Baptists, Evangelicals, Protestants, Muslims, Jews each have their own celebrations. The plurality of churches, the separation of religions puzzles and disturbs them. They ask: "Why are there so many religions, so many denominations, so many individual ways to approach God?" It is a very good question, quite naturally posed one day or another when one is growing up, but here it is notoriously in peril of producing confusion. The environment here is such that it is easy to try out all sorts of things and to give oneself all sorts of reasons for making comparisons while remaining a spectator. Separation from liberty can very easily become a separation from responsibility. What remains is only the indifference of certainty without substance.

There are two ways in which we may approach this religious division: one of these is like a place of doubt, obscurity, extreme fragility, leading nowhere except to greater confusion. I decline to choose, or rather, I try everything; I am at home everywhere and nowhere. I fool myself about my broad-mindedness. My life has no point of reference and my face is a mask. I am fatherless, and I am dying of it. And certainly, this attitude is not absent in prison.

The other way is like a place of encounter, of religious challenge, an encouragement to look farther. Outside, beyond the prison walls, it is very easy, and no doubt dangerous, to forget about other people's beliefs when they do not interfere with our own. Ignoring geographical proximity and the evidence of the facts, each church can close itself up coolly within its walls and strive to live as if it were alone. (But of course what I have described is no longer a church; it is fanaticism, a sect.) Here at Rikers, as a chaplain and a Catholic, I do not experience a single day in which I am not confronted by the harshness, the wounds, the incontrovertible evidence of religious division. In this situation there is no way of avoiding the question, or ducking a response to it.

This diversity is the subject of endless discussions here. Is it a peculiarity of America, this land that is so hospitable, a free country in every respect, or is it an impenetrable mystery of our human ways? The presence, personified by the chaplains, of so many open routes, possible changes, different allegiances, unwillingly adds to the obscurity, strangeness and sadness of the prison. One sees only the forms and the framework, but there is no available contact with the base.

If we cannot pretend, at least, based on our personal encounters, to have definitive, unifying answers to these huge questions that divide us, if we know and see that every church, here or elsewhere, wants to open itself to dialogue and encounter, if there are already "apprenticeships" in ecumenism, can we still, even at Rikers, enter to the best of our abilities into this kind of approach to one another, implying, as it does, confidence, knowledge and truthfulness?

Without fracturing the initial overture, we need to have a clarity of conviction in order, first, to situate ourselves, to know who we are and to unite with all that is happening today in this painful and urgent birth of unity, "that the world may believe."

We begin with respect, the silence of welcome, and the ambition to work in faith; we try to capture the thing that gives life to the others. The others think differently, act differently, live differently. They have a different faith; they hold themselves apart and are the rich witnesses of a different world.

If there is a place where it is necessary to mobilize good will, spiritualities, and consciences, it is certainly in this place! To get beyond simple conviviality, where people acknowledge one another just because they are supposed to, because they are in business together, and to try to approach the state of dialogue where real encounter takes place, a meeting that happens not for the sake of gain but for the sake of moving together, not for defense or attack but for growth, is an enormous challenge for all of us. No one here can avoid this challenge. Thus the test of the chaplain is his or her credibility and effectiveness, like that of any other man or woman who is the bearer of a belief. How do we function in our lives? What really counts for us?

As chaplains of different denominations we are a kind of United Nations on Rikers Island. Each one of us as a representative of a different religion has a potential for division or unity. We cross one another's path in the hallways, we share offices, we sometimes meet the same people, who want to talk to each of us, we have meetings together. We all claim to be men or women of God. If we end up men or women of the system, focusing only on rights, rules, regulations, I.D. cards and numbers, something important is lost, and this is very sad. Our words and our deeds can bury our message.

Sometimes this happens and everything peters out in platitudes. The religious people involved go astray and transform themselves into a secular administration, an organization devoid of passion and of vision. This is a judgment on our false peace and our drawing back from conflict. Ecumenism has been forgotten. It is true that the title of chaplain does not automatically guarantee deep faith. I say this all the more freely since I am a member of the tribe and cannot exempt myself from the collective contributions and deficiencies of all of us.

Sometimes, on the other hand, there are moments of real grace—encounters and the providence of brothers and sisters coming from other religious traditions. We take time to acknowledge one another and how we relate to God. The terse American way of saying things doesn't prevent genuine friendship, brotherhood and love. I recall a commemoration of Martin Luther King, Jr., and a week of prayer for Christian unity, celebrated each year, in which each denomination's door was open to all. I recall memorial services for C.O.'s or inmates who had passed away. In these, a divided group became, at least for a moment, one spirit, one mind. Beautiful people can be found in all traditions.

Within a varied group of men and women who are living their faith there are always these "summit meetings," in which there is a great deal of purification. Our way of looking at things is forced to expand; we must dig beneath appearances. There is the logic of natural reason, there is the past, the impenetrable mystery of our birth: being born a Jew, a Muslim, a Protestant, a Catholic, being born into this family, that country. Finally, there is the mystery of God in the midst of all our woundedness.

No doubt, for all of us here, the most obvious pilgrimage to the sources of a living ecumenism is that to the God of Abraham, the father of believers and cornerstone of faith. This reminds us of what the pope said to Muslims at Casablanca in 1985, expressing to them the richness of our common roots and also "the mystery of our fundamental differences about which, we believe, God will give us clarity some day." The prophetic meeting at Assisi in October 1986 with representatives of all religions "not to pray together but to be together to pray" had an impact even at Rikers. Many people spoke to me about it. They asked me for prayers from other religions. I cut them out of the *New York Times*.

The crying evidence of the prison, in the midst of so many frustrations, is that people who are dispossessed, in exile, thirsting for forgiveness, find themselves in the optimum place for embracing Life, for encountering others." I don't want prison to be the end of the world for me," says Tony. "I want to be able to start over."

"On Ash Wednesday I went to court and pleaded guilty. I thought that was a very good day to do it," says John.

To know how to lose everything is to know how to gain everything. "Since I have been in nothingness, I find that I lack nothing," said St. John of the Cross. Jesus, the universal expert in humanity.

Despite obstacles, suffering and evidence that the road is still very long, nothing forbids us to look far ahead, to investigate the hearts of men and women, to search the heart of God, to try to go "where everything converges. " One flock, one shepherd . . . the dream, hope, and urgency of today . . . the privilege and reality of tomorrow.

9

SUICIDE WATCH

The saying that we are members one of another is
not a mere pious formula to be repeated in church
without any meaning; it is a literal truth; for
though the rich end of town can avoid living with
the poor, it cannot avoid dying with the poor.
— George Bernard Shaw

*A*t regular intervals near the major holidays, especially at Christmas, the word *suicide* is spoken. The DOC circulates pamphlets on suicide prevention. In addition, throughout the year, in every block and every dormitory, there are prisoners who are employed solely for the purpose of surveillance, to be there and to prevent suicides. Every fifteen minutes they are supposed to see everyone and walk through the whole area. Suicide watch is a job here, because the prison touches the heart of existence; it unlocks the fundamental questions of meaning, life and death, and so finds within its walls the massive failure called suicide. I do not have current statistics. I only remember a report of a few years ago which mentioned more than eighty suicides at Rikers within ten years. I do not have the exact figures, but I have faces, conversations, facts that go on haunting me, witnesses to the fissures that run through all the "why" of the world. I can understand why the DOC continues to be very sensitive and concerned about these issues, and I understand that as chaplains we are in a very good place to see the implications. We see not merely scars on wrists or throat, pains in the stomach or wherever you please; there are also conversations and often the giddy darkness of nothingness when action has finally achieved its purpose, has succeeded. What has gone before, that it should turn out this way? That is the question that obsesses those who are left behind.

"When you're dead, you're free." That sentence on a poor little piece of paper, as a final testament, is the sign of a radical failure. I remember a prisoner who wanted to paint himself on canvas, the way he saw himself. He portrayed himself on his knees on the ground, with an enormous box on his shoulders, supported by his hands. On top of the box there was a dead bird with broken wings. "Those are my dreams," he said. And around him, the earth was cracking and gaping. The painting, in its naivety, told everything: abandonment, solitude, fatigue, a sentence of death.

I have always considered it a normal responsibility of a priest

to bring the news, to want to be present with family or friends
at the moments of parting or bereavement, when everything is
reduced to the ultimate and the essential, when a whole group
is besieged by pain. When I was in a parish outside the prison,
I used to do that voluntarily, as a simple obligation, not out of
a taste or attraction for it. I found it natural, without any kind
of patronizing, not to leave people alone with their sorrow. This
was not to "de-dramatize" death or lessen its impact, but to be
with people who needed someone. For example, I was with a
grandfather who asked to see his little girl one last time before
closing his eyes forever; the act permeated the room and had
an impact on all who were there. That man had finished his
course. He departed in submission, in dignity, filled with a
mighty love. The whole human world could fix its rendezvous
here.

I find it impossible to find that kind of rationality, substance
and universality when a suicide happens at the prison. There
are no words, no possible attitude, to tell a family that a prisoner
has put an end to his life. To do this, as prescribed, in the
company of two correctional officers, is to enter into a world of
excess and abjectness, for we are nothing but one of the implac-
able moments in a frozen chain. My memories are full of cries
and endless pain, shattering the crystal of the word *humanity*. A
priest is far from being immune to fear, hesitation and doubt.
Only one answer can be and must be found and found again
without ceasing: It is only Jesus who has taken the last place,
who has been able to penetrate to the bottom of the "victory"
of hell and the nausea of nothingness.

Let me give just two examples. The first is not about a prisoner, but it remains with me as a symbol of today's world, without any distinction of conditions. This was a C. O. who was cut
down during the night with his own gun, far from home. In such
a case a captain from DOC is supposed to be present when the
family is told. After a lot of effort to locate the family—it was
Sunday, and the people were not at home—we finally made
contact with them. When we told them the news, which they
received without flinching, they had only one question: "In case
it was suicide, does the family receive compensation from the
DOC?" At that moment, in that place, without even time to

think, there surfaced another "fault" on top of all the others of that night: the lack of respect.

The second incident happened around Christmas. His name was José. He was from Guatemala. I knew him. We had talked together several times. They found him, early in the morning, hanging in his cell. This time, again, we had a lot of trouble getting in contact with the family. The building was very large, and there was no name on the mailbox. There was no way of finding the super. Quite by accident, as I was getting ready to leave with the two C. O. s, I noticed someone walking down the street who looked a lot like our inmate. I stopped him and asked: yes, he was José's brother. He was coming home from work. I told him who I was and that I had come especially to speak to him about José. He asked us to come upstairs to his flat. His wife was there; their two children were playing. There was a lighted Christmas tree. We came into that quiet world of simple joy and turned it upside down. I remember the father's action when he realized what had happened. He got up, walked straight to the Christmas tree and turned it off. The children watched, understanding without another word. The darkness in their house was the darkness in their hearts.

In the face of that pasture for the steeds of evil and of failure, which is the latent tragedy of the prison, it is certain that not everything can be charged to the account of a system that is powerless to penetrate actions and motives. In decisions such as those that lead to suicide, there is more going on than questions of environment or external conditions, even if these play their part. Any power, especially one with a variety of means at its disposal, must always place controls on its force and impact. Inside the prison, it will always be at pains not to be seen as the enemy or at least the adversary. I will not try to comment on the tyrannies that are always possible where people are fallible and all of them imperfect. Nor am I trying to shove off all the crimes on a society that is already too badly wounded. But I believe that the challenge here, as in many other places, is whether humanity is in regression or progression. Everything that happens at Rikers, every witness who cares to think about what he or she has seen, produces a plethora of urgent invitations to make structural progress while changing the atmosphere; to act where one is, in concert with others; to meditate on the mystery of the choice before all of us, that is, to live in hope or to sink down in darkness.

Once more the antidote to all the fatalities is a perspective, a look upward. A bird that is charmed by a snake cannot sing. To escape from the fascination of the absolute void, of the incomprehensible, requires the kind of struggle that has something in common with the wisdom of the saints. It means valuing the kind of realism that is called spiritual. The crushed and broken hearts in prison are not out of reach of the Bible. On the contrary, everything we learn there about God points toward them.

10

SOME ELEMENTS OF A PRISON THEOLOGY

What desert, or rather what Kafkaesque castle is it in which a Christian has lost the sense of forgiveness while keeping that of sin! For the worst thing which can befall a person is to believe in sin, whereas there is no other Credo than that of the remission of sins. It is really the reversal of the spiritual world. A civilization where the preaching of sin has replaced that of pardon, where a narrow juridical notion of the defense of society outwardly coincides with a pitiless practice of competition and profit—such a civilization without generosity is the territory not only of unreal guilt but of a lack of exculpation.

—Paul Ricoeur

If you look at a detailed map of New York, on which the street numbers are given and monuments identified, Rikers Island in the East River with its more than 13,000 inhabitants is simply a white space without any detail. A parish in these parts has no visibility; it does not exist in the official structures of the archdiocese, even though the approval of the chancery is required for the appointment of Roman Catholic chaplains. Every year the seminarians come to Rikers, meeting with prisoners once a week and thus beginning to make contact with them. Their time is too much taken up by other things for them to be able to join in our celebrations. They are in training here. Their presence is marginal but undoubtedly not without its interest for future pastors. This parish is no longer required to keep any registers. For example, it suffices if baptisms are registered at a neighboring parish on the outside. I have already done that a number of times. And there is one pleasant feature here: no collections.

Despite the deficiencies and impossibilities, to the extent that one gets close to the place one quickly sees that its ecclesial character is incontestable. What difference does a place in itself make when we find here men and women who live, believe, suffer and pray every day? Indifference or a superficial glance at the whole is not adequate. There is too much human reality at Rikers for the chaplaincy to be merely a job, a task like any other within an administration that is often rigid and abstract, as if it were condemned to impose itself on others: "Prisons have always existed and will always exist. . . . You just have to put up with it. . . . Whether you like it or not, prisons are a business like any other. . . . You can make a career here and even build a future." But without getting involved in the commentaries of sociologists, legal experts or even the ordinary citizens of New York, let me say that it is the church at Rikers that interests me, the flesh and blood people I meet every day and who, little by little, have become my theological *locus*, a land of the gospel, a land of surprises mediated by all its histories, its faces and voices.

The Trappists of Holy Cross Abbey at Berryville, Virginia, have a large library. I have been there often in the course of a number of visits to the abbey, in surroundings that are remarkably different and, for that very reason, extraordinarily helpful for my ordinary life. Their lamp burns all night. They are praying. They are an oasis. At present, as I am writing, they are involved in litigation with a group of promoters who want to build a golf course right next to the monastery. At stake is a lot of money and a lot of noise against the reality of a prayerful presence. We hear that the case has been delayed. These people do not understand that the monks in this place have dedicated themselves to a life of prayer which prevents the world from suffocating. The monks are the anti-stress factor, and such things are not for sale.

At any rate, I was hoping to find some literature about prisons in their library, to see whether they had any studies, any "theology of prisoners" based on the Bible, stemming from the experience of incarceration, a theology for the poorest of the poor, so to speak, a theology of liberation worked out together with them, and growing out of the realities in which they are immersed. I thought I would be able to go straight to the source and would easily find what I was looking for. But instead, little by little, I became aware that on these particular questions there was a veritable famine of articles and of material. I had to change my tack. So I undertook to collect some references from an index, but still without finding what I was really looking for. I only had four questions in my head, by way of a methodical beginning: (1) What people in the Bible were put in prison? (2) Why? (3) What happened to them? (4) What (good or bad) consequence resulted?

I learned that imprisonment was not used as a punishment in the ancient world; it was only employed to hold someone awaiting trial. There were no prisons, as distinct edifices. Rooms or dungeons, as places of detention, were simply parts of or additions to other buildings. Joseph and his companions were kept in a dungeon, probably in Potiphar's house (Gen 40:15, 41:40). Samson was undoubtedly imprisoned close to a place

where people were working. He had to turn a mill wheel (Jg
16:21-25). Micah was kept in Ahab's palace (1 Kg 22:27) as
Hosea was in the palace of the king of Assyria (2 Kg 17:4).
Jeremiah had some variety: Jonathan's private house, a guard
room, and even a cistern where he was expected to die. John
the Baptist was kept in a fortress, not to wait for trial or exe-
cution, but to keep him away from the people. The place where
the apostles were imprisoned was quite close to the Temple.
Paul was confined in a private house. He mentions prison as
one of the perils of his apostolate (2 Cor 6:5). It often involved
chains as well (Acts 16:26).[1]

But what appears most clearly in the Bible is that many men
and women of God — judges, prophets and apostles — had this
experience of the power of other people over them. And very
often this place of ultimate testing became a place of revelation,
of the presence of God, as the story of Joseph shows (Gen 37-
47).

Joseph's brothers, jealous of their father's affection for him,
decided to kill Joseph. He was thrown into a pit and then sold
to one of Pharaoh's Egyptian officials, Potiphar. Joseph rebuffed
the advances of Potiphar's wife because he would not sin against
his God. Then the woman gave false testimony against Joseph,
and he was thrown into prison.

But God did not abandon Joseph; he enjoyed a position of
favor within the prison. He got along well with his guards, helped
the other prisoners and interpreted the dreams of two of Pharaoh's employees, who were also in prison. After more than two
years of detention, Joseph himself was called to Pharaoh to
interpret his disturbing dreams. When he heard Joseph, Pharaoh
realized that Joseph had the spirit of God.

Pharaoh put Joseph in charge of all of Egyptian agriculture.
Joseph stored up grain as a provision against the years of famine
that were coming. He welcomed his brothers, after first behaving
very rudely to them. It was a time of testing, a time of emotion.
He reunited his whole family in Egypt, where they experienced
the blessing of God, forgiveness and the hope of the promised
land.

I went on thus with Samson in the book of Judges, some

prophets in Chronicles and in the books of Kings, and finally came to Jeremiah.

Jeremiah is a gold mine, an extremely rich model, precious and unique for everything that goes on in prison. His loneliness, his depression, his sensitivity, his distress, his clinging to the thread of life that led on through all his darkness and suffering, his tragic destiny, his powerlessness, the anticonformist attitude he maintained, the God who erupted so rudely into his life . . . all these have brought me to speak of him very often to the prisoners.

Studying Jeremiah, seeing him struggling at the "center of misery" as well as at the "center of mystery" is already a doorway, an exit from here. I believe that all the misery of the world, all the cries, all the patience of every individual are recorded and mingled in Jeremiah. He is a witness. He is a beacon. He does more than he seems to do: he "is." He is impaled. This man of peace and tender friendship knew nothing on this earth but war and exile.

I admit it. It is only since I have been at Rikers that I have discovered Jeremiah, that he has become someone for me. It is as if we need certain situations and experiences to recover a message. As the prisoners often say, one after another, at those moments when the light begins to dawn: "But all that is what's happening to me right now!" Even if we cannot push the identification too far, even if we have to respect limits and make adjustments, they understand very fast. They are in a state of receptivity that is rarely found anywhere else.

And then I turned to Paul, with his letters from captivity: Ephesians, Colossians, Philippians, Philemon.[2] Paul knew more than one captivity. Clement of Rome counted seven of them. The book of Acts, which mentions several, has no allusion to an arrest of the apostle at Ephesus. We only know that he had been in grave danger there, which he refers to as his "fighting with the beasts" (1 Cor 15:32). Only Paul's letter to the Philippians furnishes us with precise details of that captivity, during which the letter was written. We also have his note to Philemon regarding a fugitive slave who had become a brother, whom Paul recommends warmly to his former master. We also know of his journey to Rome, in which he was a prisoner from beginning to end: arrested at Jerusalem, imprisoned at Caesarea, he was detained for two years awaiting a trial which did not take place. In spite of well-founded hopes that he would be freed, the possibility of martyrdom was never out of his view.

All these periods of forced immobility were for Paul the occasion for reflection and an opportunity to present himself in full confidence as the "privileged revealer of the mystery of Christ to the Gentiles," in solidarity with the other apostles. For him, his captivity was part of the plan of God. Called for the salvation of the Gentiles, he is now a prisoner of Christ Jesus for their sake (Eph 3:1). The sufferings he endures in his captivity are completing his work. After having been a minister of the church by his apostolic work, he completes, in his apparent inactivity, those things suffered by Christ (Col 1:24).

In captivity Paul remains the apostle who is always free. His presence at Rome, even in prison, marks a resumption of activity for the sake of the whole community. His disciples and friends find in Paul a powerful encouragement. He takes advantage of his personal influence for the interests of the gospel: "What has happened to me has really served to advance the gospel, so that it has become known throughout the whole praetorian guard and to all the rest that my imprisonment is for Christ; and most of the brethren have been made confident in the Lord because of my imprisonment, and are much more bold to speak the word of God without fear" (Phil 1:12–14). Even in his absence the apostle remains attentive to the daily sufferings of the Christian community, as well as to the passing crazes that endanger the purity of their faith. His captivity has made him understand that he is approaching the end of his career. He is finishing, in truth and fullness, what began one day on the road to Damascus. Jesus found him, and he found Jesus. Nothing can touch him now. He is free. This is not pride in oneself, but total confidence in Christ.

Paul's imprisonment left him uncertain to the very end about the outcome. But that does not matter; he has renounced everything for the perfect joy of union with Christ. He says so to the Philippians: for him, now, "to live is Christ."

Approaching Paul from the prisoner's point of view does not prevent, but on the contrary encourages us to look at his life as one wide open to unbelief and to borderline people. I like the fact that he went to Athens, and to the areopagus. I like the fact that his letters and his thought take their departure from other people's questions and the chains he endures, that he works in order not to be a burden to anyone, that he has a criminal past and a thousand disappointments. The conversion of Paul, the reflections of Paul the captive, are a fertile source for Rikers.

But to return to my prison theology, an inventory, even if systematic and detailed, drawn from the whole Bible still left me hungry. I did not see where to go with it. I had not been able to bring it together as a coherent whole. I felt I was marking time, and on the other hand that I had an inkling of something important. I asked some questions of my friends here and there, and wrote some letters, but again without result. How was I going to deal with what I was living every day in the "church in prison"? And then one day I stumbled on an article entitled "Custody and the Ministry to Prisoners."[3] I would like at this point to summarize the article, adding some commentary, because it gave me, black on white, just what I was looking for everywhere, without knowing exactly what it was.

First of all, the author establishes a point pregnant with meaning and understood so well by many friends here. It seems that neither the Bible nor the church's tradition has anything particular or specific to say about prison, for the simple and unique reason that prison, normally, should not exist.

There is nothing in the Mosaic law about imprisonment. Punishment, by the law of talion, consists of a penalty equal to the offense: eye for eye, tooth for tooth. There is a death penalty, too. One is obliged to make restitution. And if that is impossible, the debtor becomes a slave. There is also the penalty of flagellation. The whole system presupposes a society based on strong religious convictions, as well as a society that accepts slavery.

Nevertheless, from the beginning we read about people who are put in prison: those who are subsequently to be judged, or else those who are dangerous and from whom society needs protection. That very quickly becomes an established custom, even if, theoretically, prison is something abnormal, unknown to the law. It is considered a manifestation of an imperfect society and of circumstances governed by sin.

It is on this basis that we are to understand the messianic promise of Isaiah 61:1, which Jesus makes his own at the beginning of his public life: "The Spirit of the Lord is upon me. . . . He has sent me to proclaim liberty to the captives, and the opening of the prison to those who are bound." It should be noted that this is not an envoy sent to act, but to proclaim: to proclaim the end of the established disorder a prison is. The Messiah is to announce liberation from all shackles and from all chains.

Revolutions in every age have always included among their first actions the opening of prisons. This is not to establish anarchy, but because prisons are the sharpest sign of the unjust society the revolution intends to change.

In the New Testament and the church's tradition, a ministry to prisoners has always been recognized and encouraged. Since the days of Jesus there has been a solidarity in principle between Christians and every victim of human sin, whether voluntary or involuntary. "Remember those who are in prison, as though in prison with them" (Heb 13:3).

There has never been, in the tradition, any trace of embarrassment regarding the attitude one ought to take toward prisoners, as if there were some kind of choice to be made between punishing and forgiving, or as if this ministry risked interfering too much with a judgment already given.

Little by little, in the course of history, something happened as the church realized that it was not merely responsible for ministry to prisoners, but was involved in the organization of prisons themselves, and in their reform and betterment.

It is not possible here to go into the details of this history, its evolution, or the debates that are still going on. Christians who serve in prisons are involved in them in every way, in the name of what their faith demands of them. Even if the Bible says nothing about the purpose of prisons, there are principles that remain as beacons for our conduct and the way we view them. Several things are certain:

1. A ministry to prisoners, if it is Christian, is not just a gratuitous and inoffensive gesture simply to be tolerated. It is demanded by Jesus: "I was in prison and you came to visit me." It is found at the beginning of the church's apostolate. This

ministry is not specialized; it is nothing exceptional. It is only one ministry among others. Still, in our day it is neither very common nor widespread. A hospital has a much better chance of finding a chaplain.

2. Prisons are not the only places where we can find dehumanization or absence of liberty. An unemployed person, an undocumented alien, a vagrant, a prostitute—all are victims in differing degrees, in one way or another, of pernicious circumstances that result from human sin. My experience at Rikers from the very earliest days showed me this quite clearly. People are alike, and I could meet on the street the whole complex of people I see here. I believe that I received that perception as a shock and an encouragement: a shock because of the human vulnerability and fragility (someone asked a prisoner: "Why are you in prison?" and the prisoner answered, echoing Thoreau, "Why aren't you?"); encouragement because of the possibility of contact and the promise of a life that is never completely extinguished.

3. This ministry has a dimension proper to itself. How can one accept the liberty for captives promised by Christ when one is in prison? What chaplain has not had to ask himself or herself that question?

Proclaiming liberty for captives means announcing a situation in which there are no more prisons. But is that something that is already accomplished or will it only come later? As with the reign of God, we need to answer: "It is here and not yet here." It is here in those transparent moments, for example, in certain meetings, celebrations, retreats, and events when, if the group seems to be something more than the individuals who make it up, one sees, realizes, understands the significance of the words *repentance*, *conversion*, *communion*. Even if it is always necessary to make a discernment between instinctive impulses, passing emotions, and a work of the Spirit that creates a rebirth of the brothers and sisters in and through their crosses and their joys, these blessed moments are flashing instants in which there is no more prison. On such a day we travel far, and the unthinkable becomes realistic: a society without prisons.

The liberty for captives is not yet here when there is no other possible alternative for criminals except prison.

It is not a question of a pendulum balancing between utopia and good, solid common sense, but of knowing how to nourish within oneself the certainty that prisons will one day cease to exist because human beings will have accepted God's view of them, because they will have found their center.

The article speaks of experience as a means of fortifying within oneself this certainty of the end of prisons. This goes to the depth of our hearts, with their heavy resistance and acquiescence. The keys are personal repentance, generosity and a living church that is discovering and following its own road.

We are here far removed from the ideas about prisons to be found in the newspapers or in the media. Without devaluing in any way the attempts that are being made here or there to improve or change approaches to correction, we still need to say that the truth about each of us must be plumbed in all its depth if we are to arrive at total liberation. When someone has reached absolute bottom, the point at which he or she has nothing more to lose, the church, which has in itself the treasures of life, is the only organ that is truly a friend and capable of response. Every other presence, every other voice may fill the air with music and the ocean with waves, but in the final analysis it can only be incomplete and leave us unsatisfied. Because they have been wounded at the heart, because they have seen too much, prisoners will be quick to discern watered-down reality, the poseur within the witness and even the traitor in the faithful friend. Many have surprised me with their quick understanding. There is an intelligent instinct in the prison because it is the instinct of the poor.

There are living and explosive forces here, full of question marks for a society that is too simplistic. How can I be a member of a society which has already punished me so much, which has already told me so many lies? I am reminded of that great film from the fifties, "La Strada." If so many prisons are full of Zampanos, hunting tigers roaring in their cages, we need just as many Gelsominas to explode their armor and free the child within the most hardened of them. In a situation of dereliction, malice and intense anger, only the gospel is able to disarm, to restore and to make possible a new dawn. The story of John the Baptist in prison, of the criminal on the cross alongside Jesus, the original words of Christ and of all the witnesses who followed him pierce the walls and bars of Rikers. Here is the fragility of an elementary and vague unbelief that does not know where or to whom to turn. Here is the confused and cringing sound of faith finding whatever gestures it can, reaching out for relationship and for simplicity, and seeking in darkness and the desert for living words. "My mother always said to me: 'You are going to end up killing me!' Now here I am in prison, and yesterday she died. She died because of me! Please help me!" (These were the words of an inmate to the community during Mass.) A wise person has said: "Something is lacking in anyone who has never known unhappiness, illness or prison."

So a prison theology cannot be a theology of ordinary days, of the necessary commonness of existence that is called normal, that is recognized and naturally integrated into society. That is not to say that such an existence is without problems or surprises; the world is too full of mystery for that. In any case, in prison, it very quickly becomes a theology of the cross and the resurrection against the forces of death, a theology of conscience, a theology of life. It takes its departure from that massive reality of suffering and sin, from the radical questions. That is why it can only originate with these people, with those who know or have known what it means to be in prison. Jesus' concern moved beyond people's actions to their hearts: "Your faith has saved you." And in prison, everything boils down to the story of that faith.

If the history of human violence, however deep and however real, goes back to the world's earliest beginnings, back to Cain, it ends at the cross. To triumph over it, nothing less was needed than the death of God. And Jesus died between two criminals! I ask myself whether the "happy Good Friday" I heard this year at Rikers is not trying to say exactly that. The men associated with his suffering and death were criminals. One of them made his exit in a divine way, moving from defeat to absolute victory, the first one to be saved, the first one canonized by the death of Christ. The other enclosed himself in his own refusal.

It is also for that reason that prison theology, which heals by fixing its view on the cross of Christ, cannot fail to include the past and thus, in a great many cases, the innocent sufferers, the victims. The silence of graves, the sorrow of broken families, the contempt for collective or private rights—no one can trivialize or lightheartedly accept this state of affairs. To return to communion with God and others, even if it has nothing to do with human justice or the world's opinion, cannot involve an avoidance of responsibility for restitution or reparation, what the church calls expiation. It is the rediscovery of the treasure so often hidden in every life, namely, conscience. Sharing to the extent possible in the irremediable act one has committed, bearing the marks of it before God, is also the way of salvation. This is one of our lasting reflections at Rikers. We never have communal prayer without mentioning the victims.

Here I might insert, as a counterpoint or alternative view by way of balance, the words of a father whose daughter had been strangled by a sadist. He found the strength to say to the newspaper people who were storming his house in New York: "Don't waste your time replacing love with hatred."

The time lived in prison is dead time, or time alone with thoughts, with the coming and going of faith and its appearances, of refusal and acceptance, of doubt and conviction. "Even in prison, if you are with God, you are a giant," says Jimmy. In the streets, in the prisons, there are surprises: unawaited presences where God is hidden or revealed.

For those in prison, far removed from the normal responsibilities which are also the sign of one's dignity, the leaden casing of evil and sin presses down horribly. I have already spoken about Jacob's struggle in the dark. We have no grip. The weight of silence makes us burn to hear something. We are obsessed with time. Everybody here watches the clock or the calendar. The same questions are raised again and again: "How long have you been here? How much time did you get? When is your trial?" Life in prison could easily be represented by the hands of a clock. And yet, my task is to say that life is not reducible to the hands of a clock, that it can change, even for a prisoner. You know, you see that evil exists. You have your feet in the mud here. But you have eyes, too. You see that life is something quite different, that it is much greater, that there is someplace else.

Should one search for God in sincerity or just turn over a

new leaf at the lowest cost? There are moments of truth, those of life and of prayer really shared. There are signs, words, and gestures that do not deceive, people used to playing rough who get broken along the way and lay themselves bare.

I have prayed in C 95 with a man, still young, who had killed his mother. It was a crazy, horrible crime. He was very pale and looked like a lost man, crushed by the misery that had fallen upon him. He complained of constant headache and said he had nothing left. Today he left Rikers; he went to an upstate prison to serve his sentence. I do not know whether he has kept his faith and spiritual life, but when I was face to face with him, I knew by his attention and the quality of what he shared with me that we were in what believers call the invisible kingdom.

A priest from Mexico confided to me one day his strong conviction that "mentally ill people always understand when it's a question of God."

But aren't there good reasons to be skeptical? moments when the confessions sound false or penitence is only a pretence? The test, as in everything, is endurance. When you are building on rock, you have to begin very small.

In these conversations there are not only falling tears or bleeding hearts. There is often also an unconscious desire to equate human justice with God's justice. "Because I am being punished by human beings, I am being punished by God; God has put me in here for some reason." And here again I have to help them understand that people can punish, but God can forgive, and that God knows that I have sinned even if people wipe it from the record. Human justice and God's justice don't necessarily overlap. I repeat this to them over and over again. Teresa of Avila said, "I know when I commit a grave fault. If I put myself in hell, I can't hide it from myself. I don't need other people's opinion to know it and to judge myself."

FORGIVENESS

Now I come to the heart of my theological reflections on prisons. I have already touched on it, but I want to speak of it in a more concise and developed way, because it is only the lack of it that causes the death of everyone at Rikers or elsewhere. I am speaking of *forgiveness*. Even the Christian who is "just," who is no one special, is first of all a forgiven sinner. Forgiveness is my passion. After twenty-eight years of priesthood, what I still value most, what I have really discovered here, is forgiveness. From the depth of my soul and conscience, I would say that it is this that brings me to the center of what the church entrusted to me in 1961. For me, as for the majority of people, I am sure that it is both the place where the enemy is vanquished and the locus of the greatest revelation of God.

There is the experience of pardon in the Old Testament.[4] It came to pass that God "was sorry and grieved to the heart" to see the wickedness of human beings on earth (Gen 6:5–6), but even so, after the deluge, God announced: "I will never again curse the ground because of human beings" (Gen 8:21). Even before it is pity, God's forgiveness is a will to give life.

After the episode of the golden calf, when Moses begged God to pardon the people even at the cost of his own life (Ex 32:32), God responds with a self description: "A God merciful and gracious, slow to anger, and abounding in steadfast love and faithfulness, keeping steadfast love for thousands, forgiving iniquity and transgression and sin, but who will by no means clear the guilty" (Ex 34:6–7). God is capable of anger, but anger does not define who God is. The explanation of God's anger is the weight of sin, its capacity for destruction and death, all at work in creation. But there is no proportion between that power of death and the strength of life and salvation which comes to us in Jesus (Rom 8:38–39).

Abraham's great prayer of intercession for Sodom (Gen 18:23–32) and Amos's prayer for Israel in mortal danger (Amos 7:2–6) not only express a profound notion of human solidarity, but are both provoked by a divine intervention. For example: "Shall I hide from Abraham what I am about to do?"(Gen 18:17). Hosea's experience was exceptional. God ordered this prophet to take back his adulterous wife even though, according to the letter of the law, she should have been put to death together with her lover (cf. Jn 8:5). In the demand that Hosea forgive his wife we see a partial revelation of who God is: I am God and not a man, the Holy One in your midst, and I will not come to destroy" (Hos 11:9). It is impossible to know how Hosea came to understand that what was true of him was true also of

God, that here was a God who suffered and was in pain because of the infidelity of God's people. He saw that God's forgiveness is a fact. For the sinner, it is always an encounter, a new birth.

In forgiving, God says who God is. "With everlasting love I will have compassion on you ... for this is like the days of Noah to me: as I swore that the waters of Noah should no more go over the earth, so I have sworn that I will not be angry with you and will not rebuke you" (Is 54:8-9).

The people who heard and who wrote these words were a people who were vanquished, deported, dishonored. They had lost everything, their king, their temple, their law, their land, and suddenly they had realized that salvation was at hand. Their attitude was not so much an imaginary leap into the future as a certainty that their God was active on their behalf. If a ray of hope remains in the midst of catastrophe, it comes from this God who does not accept the sin, but wills that the sinner should live (Ezek 18:23-32).

And, of course, there is Jesus and the experience of forgiveness. One of the notable features of the beginning of the gospels, in the scenes with John the Baptist and Jesus, is that many sinners came to be baptized and receive pardon for their sins (Mk 1:5; Jn 3:23). It is only after the arrest of John the Baptist that Jesus moves out to proclaim the message of joy, the good news. John the Baptist announced the advent of Jesus by saying that he would be a terrible threat to sinners (Mt 3:10). Jesus proclaims that his coming is a joy for everyone (Lk 2:10). That is why he cannot remain in any one place, and always has to go elsewhere to proclaim the gospel.

"Elsewhere" means primarily among those people who have no way of knowing this good news. Concretely, sinners are those whom honest people reject and exclude, tax collectors, prostitutes and sinners. Nearly all the words of forgiveness in the gospels are addressed to sinners. Every time, that pardon changes everything. "Do you see this woman?" (Lk 7:44). Take a good look at her and you will understand who God is and what forgiveness means.

In forgiving, God tells us why God is there. Jesus goes out of his way to encounter sinners and welcomes them so warmly primarily because it is for them that he has come, and for the sick and those who have no one (Jn 5:7). If he does not come to see them, these people are condemned to perish. For Jesus' forgiveness is the revelation of sin, its power to paralyze and to kill. But death is something God cannot stand, and Jesus has come to prove this, to seek out and save that which is lost" (Lk 19:10).

To lose something, whether a sheep or a piece of silver, is a dramatic event, especially for the poor, and finding it is a joy. The gospel purposely emphasizes Jesus' intention in giving these examples: It is to respond to the accusations of those who say that he "welcomes sinners and eats with them"(Lk 15:2).

The words "your sins are forgiven" tell us what it means to receive forgiveness. It is Jesus' recognition of faith, of that personal movement toward Himself which happens in an encounter, a dialogue, a word received from someone.

"Forgive that your Father may forgive you"(Mk 11:25). "Forgive us as we forgive others" (Mt 6:12). Should you not have had mercy on your fellow servant, as I had mercy on you?" (Mt 18:33). No matter what form it takes, the Lord's command is categorical. To enter into the divine secret of forgiveness is to find oneself obligated to share it. The life saved, the healing, the end of a sentence or a condemnation cries out and proclaims itself. In chapter 18 of Matthew's gospel we see that the gospel community is founded on forgiveness. There is no real community unless all those present are willing to be brothers and sisters. The church, in its early days, lived this forgiveness. The moment of crisis was the entry of Gentiles into the Christian community. They were admitted in the name of forgiveness, the imperative law and the hope offered to all humanity.

But forgiveness may not fly in the face of justice. Anyone who pardons without weighing the injustice and seeing the evil in it forgives badly, refusing to relieve the human heart of its wickedness. But there is no justice without moderation. It is not a question of abolishing it, but of moving toward that more abundant justice that is presented in the Sermon on the Mount (Mt 5:20): "Unless your righteousness exceeds that of the scribes and Pharisees, you will never enter the kingdom of heaven." We are talking about entering into a new world, where relationships broken by evil are restored.

Forgiveness always has a collective dimension. It touches other people. We forgive that we may be forgiven (Mt 6:14–15). But we are not talking about making calculations, as if I could pay for my pardon through the pardon I give my enemy. Instead, it is a question of truthfulness. If I ought to forgive, it is because I myself need to be forgiven. I am a sinner. Moreover, every fault, no matter how secret, touches other people. Sin wounds the world, the church, the body of Christ.

Repentance is impossible unless human beings accept their responsibility before God. It begins with the words of confession: I have willed what is evil and have done it (cf. Psalm 51). This is done in openness and honesty, in interior clarity. It is impossible to con the gospel.

Christian confession liberates. Anyone who is bound by his or her mortal guilt cannot really be re-created except by a powerful word coming from outside. The "I absolve you from your sins" of the sacrament of reconciliation is that liberating word. It originates in the will to heal chosen by Jesus, the physician, a will and a choice that consisted of nothing less than taking on himself our own sickness (Mt 8:17).

If there were no pardon for the sinner or hope for a new future, I would have left Rikers long ago. What kind of hope is there in prison? When a person hits bottom, weeps, has lost everything, searches in the dark, how can we not think of forgiveness? As long as there is life and breath, I am infinitely certain that a person can change, even in prison. Sin is a hindrance to liberty, a hindrance to love, an open wound, a sickness to be given to God.

The boy whose two brothers had been violently killed, and whose other two brothers are in prison like him, lives, prays and hopes. It was he who said to me: "I have learned my lesson. I want to get out—and this time, with God."

The AIDS patients in the hospital have a lot to think about. Some of them are exhausted and have lost all their strength. Their neighbors, companions in misfortune, help them as best they can. "We are crutches for each other," says one of them.

If a human being does not know that he or she is forgiven and loved by God, if hope is cut off, that person is like a walking corpse, a breathing death. And that is the worst kind of death.

It is even worse than being killed, cut down by a firearm. Because it is final. In this short life there are some rays of light that can touch it. They come from the possibility of forgiveness the church gives. The church has a treasury of life that lasts forever. There is no failure and nothing is hopeless for those who begin to love again.

A Note on Jesus' Words in Matthew 25:36: "I Was in Prison and You Came to Visit Me"

Since my first days at Rikers I have lived through several interpretations of these words. Perhaps now it is the time to say how I understand them today. Because things are clearer now. Experience is always an ongoing education. I can never pretend to be a prison specialist. Every day is a new world. Every person is a new world. I have said it before and I will repeat it: You cannot meet a prison population; you can only meet persons.

I used to think when I started going to Rikers that Jesus could be found everywhere and in whomever in prison, that it was sufficient for a person to be a prisoner in order for him immediately to be the object of compassion. I have learned that to approach people from this angle is to wander aimlessly, to manipulate the Word of the gospel. I had to bring the stern and saving message of the gospel to everything I saw in prison. Then came the realization that here there was too much evil, too many enemies for me to deny their reality. The evidence of too many bad habits and the absence of remorse could not be hidden.

What the gospel, and especially St. Matthew says to me is that I can only hope to meet Jesus in his brothers, the least of them, his disciples who follow him in real life and profoundly in those who struggle to stand up again after they have fallen, in those who are here through an injustice. Such persons are sources of light and examples of the beatitudes. I am convinced that there are such people at Rikers Island. I will be judged by how I have responded to the grace here in this place.

No one can live without responsibility; we are all responsible for our choices. The one who chooses evil, who imprisons himself in it and keeps playing a game cuts himself off and falls into an abyss. I do not possess the last word in these situations. Even in this place of seemingly endless misery there will always be the necessary prudence, common sense and compassion. I have learned that in prison excommunication is self-inflicted by those who consciously and deliberately choose to say no. If I don't reject the evil I hear or see or do, I then reject God and his mercy. I place myself out of reach of forgiveness, which reaches out for everyone. Jesus is not everywhere. He cannot be in what is evil. Jesus is in the least of his brethren and he waits for all of us there.

NOTES

1. The above information is taken from McKenzie, *Dictionary of the Bible* (New York: Macmillan, 1965).

2. The following material on Paul relies heavily on Lucien Cerfaux, *L'Itineraire Spirituel de St. Paul* (Paris: Cerf, 1966).

3. A. E. Harvey, "Custody and the Ministry to Prisoners," *Theology* 78 (1975).

4. The following material was found under the word *pardon* in the *Dictionnaire de spiritualité* (Paris: Bauchesne, 1984).

11

TO MY CHURCH

All those who imagine they are Christians, but don't work to polish the dignity that is in human beings, to dissipate their ignorance, to break their egoism through an example of disinterestedness, to realize within human society that perfect equality which is the practical recognition of the value of the human person—all such people mistake the shadow for the substance and deceive themselves.

—Jean Jaures

It is always good to remember that the word *catholic* means "universal." There is no "us" and "them" except for those who are wicked. When at Mass the whole assembly prays "Do not look upon our sins but the faith of your church," the whole world is included. When John XXIII opened the council in 1962, he said: "The Bride of Christ prefers today to apply the remedy of mercy rather than that of severity. She wants to provide for the needs of the present time by pointing to the value of her teaching rather than by renewing condemnation."

Before his visit to the United States in September 1987, our Christian community at Rikers had written to Pope John Paul II. This came about entirely through the initiative of the inmates themselves. It was worth seeing—the care that was taken, the discussions involved in composing that letter full of respect and hope, reaching out to a living center in a society that is visible, but so often immobile. It was a beautiful letter. (It made me think of Augustine's expression: "There is a sign by which one may know whether a man or woman possesses the Holy Spirit. It is that he or she loves the church.") Some of the inmates even wrote to the upstate prisons to ask for signatures. They came by the hundreds. Some time later we received a written message of thanks through the archdiocese. (One inmate said to me, "A letter is a flower in the desert." Then he added, "A visit is a fountain.") Did they hope for a visit? They certainly did, like all the poor who have no idea of the implications of such an event, but still keep and nourish within themselves the courageous willingness of faith. If, on that day, they did not experience the human miracle, still there was communion.

It is a fact that on each of his trips, or almost all of them, the pope has a word for prisoners. We often think of John XXIII's visit in 1958 to some inmates at the Regina Coeli prison in Rome. "I put my eyes in your eyes and my heart in your heart," he said to the prisoners, this man they called good Pope John. He walked through the corridors of the prison, and ordered the barred doors opened: "Don't shut them up while I'm here. They are God's children." Echoing that incident, one prisoner wanted to write to the Vatican in the name of his buddies, "Suffering is neither Catholic nor Protestant nor Jewish nor Muslim. Suffering is everywhere. We thank you, Holy Father, for coming to meet it."

There was also John Paul II's visit to Ali Agca, the man who attacked him in St. Peter's Square. He called that day "a historic one in my life, as a man, as a Christian and as bishop of Rome." And he added: "The Lord gave me the grace to allow us to meet one another as men and brothers."

There can be no doubt that the church has a specific mission in the prison world. I have regarded it as a task of basic building, from the ground up. The church holds the keys of life. Its visibility, its actions have a thousand forms, a thousand ways of being effective, a thousand resources. One sees them or does not see them. But when it comes to the prison, to the beacon the church represents here, at the door that swallows the better and the worse, I would say that its visible reality has a special dimension, and that its credits are often very clearly written.

Because there is so much darkness here, so many wounds and so many cries, the appeals for help are solely directed to the church, even if, for very good reason, their source is mired in confusion and extreme weakness. To say to each one that he or she is unique and irreplaceable, willed and desired from eternity, that God is Father and Mother to him or her, that there is a pity, a love, a plan at work from all eternity, that there is a place reserved in which the word *blessed* will resound forever — my God, all this is a more than blessed richness in times of famine and desert. In prison the church is quite simply the last corner, the last "green space" where everyone can return and become new again. Knowing and living that fact is enough to change one's point of view, to motivate one against discouragement, to sense which way the wind is blowing. I write with the sound of a thousand voices. My head contains albums of faces. Imprisoned brothers, disciples tossed about and yet drawn to life. It is you who are here. It is your search that is at work in these pages. It is you who are their reason and purpose. For something in you calls out, not for completion, but for discovery.

An experience is not always communicable. Outside, on the

street, interest in anything concerning prison is often simply intellectual, fleeting, determined by events, even if, alas, those events tend to repeat themselves over and over. The necessity for permanent commitment, an engagement that is open and concerned, that moves one forward, is not always as evident as it should be. And society, speaking through the newspapers and television, can quite often only express skin-deep reactions, and those reactions are irrational, fearful and defensive.

If this is the case with society, the society of the streets, still I cannot be so resigned or passive with regard to my church— my submerged church, alive and inseparable from the world. Still, I have no taste for the podium, for the massive challenges directed at that sort of a control tower. I simply want to share what fills my days and my thoughts, to speak to my church about situations that are completely on the level of what she holds most dear and most cherished, to let her hear an echo of the urgency hidden in her own heart. "Her own human weaknesses" (Paul VI, *Ecclesiam suam*) do not prevent her from being on hand for every farewell and every departure. And if she is there at parting, if she accompanies the voyager, she is also ahead of everyone else at the arrival. She is the trademark, the guarantee. And it is from within her that I am struggling and speaking to her. In a fragmented world, I know that it is she who holds the message, who can step in to heal and save—this church that says, "The worse the children are, the more we have to love them," this church to whom Jesus says, "I am with you all days."

With that much very clear, I find it is always a strange experience, and one not very easy to accept, when I discover the kind of withdrawal, silence or indifference in regard to prisons within the best groups, including clerics, who go to churches regularly. "Leave those people where they are. What can you do with criminals? They have lost all their rights. Can anything good come out of a prison?" If someone is sick, in the hospital, you can understand that, you accept it and you have sympathy. But a man or woman in a cell, in the dark, in a hole—it seems not so much a question of being suspicious of them, as of having nothing more to hear and nothing more to say. We think spontaneously that the gospel doesn't apply to these people. The devil can't be converted. And we can be so quick to identify him!

This very "upright" attitude is often the mere onset of a psychological and spiritual massacre, of long-term damage for the unfortunate object of it. One hears a thousand echoes of all that in prison. Without seeming to, and even with the best intentions and the clearest conscience, such attitudes build, support and encourage despair. How many suicides were and are rooted in them?

This may be the greatest evil I encounter here and the greatest challenge to me as a Christian and a priest: to see that when it is a question of justice, God acts differently and invites us to cooperate. Our church both knows and accepts this, so much so that it is even able to make a list. That list, chosen by the church, is the list of the names of the saints, of all the witnesses who are publicly recognized because they were able to fill their lives with the most powerful love. But on the other side, the church has no list of the damned. It does not know and cannot speak their names. What a mystery of respect for the human heart! What acknowledgment of each one's dignity to the end! If Jesus calls all sinners to conversion, and in such a radical and unhesitating manner that does not shrink from going out to the most forgotten, the most distant, how much does he, at the same time, reveal a secret to us by placing himself in such company! The identity Jesus chooses, his word as reported in Matthew 25 — "I am in prison" — overturns all our categories, day after day until the final judgment, and we have to accept and confront this for the sake of the cross, the miracle and salvation of all of us.

I think of my bishop every day, when I pray for him at Mass. For, without ignoring the person in charge of the Department of Corrections, it is the bishop who is my superior, who can call me on the carpet and ask me to report in detail. I think of him when I go to Rikers, when I see and try to understand, when I listen and try to respond. Or, more simply, I see and hear with him. It is an urgent need among all the others — and without doubting the many forms of the church's care that are expressed within an archdiocese, I need to keep my home base, to retain the character of an envoy. Those are the channels in which the vital fluid runs and through which it touches so many of the wounded in this place. So it is with my bishop that I look at the numbers and the realities that impose themselves here. For example, 105,000 men and women entered Rikers in 1987. Some of them are still here. For most, these will be the most active and daring years of their lives, the years most fraught with consequences. They will spend those years in this abandoned society, in a ferocious and directionless violence, a majority of them black, drawn from all types of minorities, all of them poor. On occasion one sees the profound wounds of racism in the midst of so many other hemorrhaging sores. What group, what "parish" outside prison has such a potential for explosion, such a thirst for answers, such a groping toward an impossible light, such need for the attentive, living, loving eyes of our church turned toward its needs?

Nathan Sharansky is well-known, not only because of his personal struggle for human rights. Returning to the "pale and complex trivialities of freedom and lost in thousands of mundane choices" during the first months after his release from prison, he said and wrote that the center of his experience of being a prisoner had been "this sense of the interconnectedness of souls." That is what enabled him to hold on; it was the great counterforce against all punishments, his strong arm against evil, his other world. I understand that very well, and I am certain that many at Rikers understand it as well—that power arising out of the depths and the abyss, the power to give ourselves to one another. It is invisible; it breaks through walls. For example, there is a convent of cloistered nuns in Europe who pray every Monday with those who are praying at Rikers. They receive *The Link*, a newsletter from our Christian community, with items in English and Spanish. They write to us regularly, and they in turn receive letters from Rikers.

Certainly a solidarity in prayer and friendship exists, and it is a comfort to us. We solicit these prayers everywhere: monasteries, retreat houses, families, friends, groups of young people and those not so young, those we know about and, most often, those who remain discreet and unknown. For example, a group of Belgians of all ages, who include among themselves blind and handicapped people, took the trouble to make their solidarity with us the theme of their Christmas preparation. There is also a woman, a volunteer prison visitor, who told me that before entering the prison walls she often had to pray a lot: "I couldn't come here otherwise," she added. Or I think of another woman who was asked: "But doesn't it bother you, going into prisons? Aren't you afraid in there?" She answered: "No, not at all. I am not afraid of anything but sin."

We know very well that the puffs of fresh air have a beginning: the strength of adoration of a community gathered before God, the grace of the communicating vessels, the diamond of the certitude of faith that penetrates us and transports us from one world to another.

On the model of Abraham pleading for Sodom, or of Moses with his arms lifted in intercession, the Christian universe is full of mystical solidarities. "The saint, the sinner, one towing the other, together, all are on the way to Jesus," as Peguy said. From the devoted silence of a Clare to the young people who are eager to come and prepare a celebration where they will sing with the prisoners, men and women are finding their unity, their integrity, their capacity to advance in their relationship with their God and in dialogue with and for others, for those who, like Elijah before Horeb, cannot bear any more of the fatigue, the thirst, the desert, and who only ask to go on to the end.

To go to Jesus by making a journey, organizing, entering into mission, into a permanent and lasting call, sets in motion a mutual commitment. The brothers and sisters with whom one has shared so much of prayer, tears and song are the same ones who depart for the upstate prisons or who get back out on the street or return to their families. They will become, with the grace of God, a more or less conscious, more or less active part of a whole. And over the years, the list of these people living in this particular diaspora has grown rather long.

At this point I need to look for a point of reference, if I am going to try to make myself understood by my church. So I will start from a statement of Vatican Council II that gives a rather complete image of the expressions of human misery: "Whatever is opposed to life itself, such as any type of murder, genocide, abortion, euthanasia, or willful self-destruction, whatever violates the integrity of the human person, such as mutilation, torments inflicted on body or mind, attempts to coerce the will itself; whatever insults human dignity, such as subhuman living conditions, arbitrary imprisonment, deportation, slavery, prostitution, the selling of women and children; as well as disgraceful working conditions, where men are treated as mere tools for profit, rather than as free and responsible persons; all these things and others of their like are infamies indeed. They poison human society, but they do more harm to those who practice them than those who suffer from the injury. Moreover, they are a supreme dishonor to the Creator" (*Gaudium et Spes*, n. 27). If the Council Fathers were writing this text today, they no doubt would include drugs, the frantic accumulation of wealth, and all the collective evils, such as weapons of death, pollution, and so on.

If we want to heal everything, we need to be able to name evil—not just keep ourselves from doing evil, but know what evil is. The beginning of realization, the beginning of knowledge, is the way out. To say without flinching, "I kill people. I feel nothing. That's all," is what the newspapers and the public rightly call the words of a monster. It justifies the existence of a special place—whether we call it a prison or not—which serves, if not for punishment, at least for confinement.

But being willing to explain the basis of our actions, without sloughing off responsibility for them, often means walking in darkness. And it means not being afraid to call names: our own, that of the devil, that of God. There is obscurity in expression, certainly, but not in substance. And when the story of a life is nothing but a story of tragedy starting at a very early age, who can expect that person not to have responses that are completely and clearly those of a "monster"? A Thérèse of Lisieux understood, in her own way, how to live "the interconnectedness of souls," the pure product of a vigorous faith and of the mercy of God.

But if there are these extremes with which reason collides and never ceases to collide, there are also all the rest, this group with whom we are now related, whether here at Rikers or somewhere upstate. In cooperation with the Office of Criminal Justice Ministries of the archdiocese and the Sisters of the Gospel, we very often make the plunge into another world, a world that is "outside" but so frequently is horribly marked by what goes on "inside" the walls of a prison. I am speaking now of the families, those who are affected first of all by what is happening far away from them. They are so distant in their powerlessness, so close in their desire: the grandmothers who have to take care of the babies, the spouses or common-law wives who cannot manage in material terms, the children who play at calling each other daddy or who call the telephone daddy because that is all they see or know of their father.

"Here, upstate," a prisoner who has been there for six years said to me, "we can't talk to each other about anything but prison stuff, things we can all see. It's impossible to talk about outside, about what is going on in our families. Who cares? Nobody would listen."

Another man has been there fifteen years. We have known each other for eight. He has maintained a lot of energy, but his life is no longer the same. His wife couldn't bear his absence; she has a boyfriend now. He has a wonderful son, partly brought up by his grandmother. This friend of mine says that he feels well in the prison, even to the point that he no longer looks forward to getting out. His philosophy now is to abstract himself from everything and practice emptiness, like a Buddhist.

"If you want to, you can learn a lot in this prison; there are some good programs here. But it is also a very efficient school for crime."

"My wife came for the weekend for a 'trailer visit.' During that time my twenty-eight-year-old son, who is a drug addict and lives in New York, took the opportunity to sell everything he could find in the house. I feel now like a piece of shit!"

"I have gone through a lot in prison these last seven years. But I would like to get out for the sake of my four children. That is what I find hardest to bear here. They need me so much!"

In three years in prison, he had never been called for a visit, had never seen the waiting room. When the C.O. did call him, he didn't believe it. After the visit, he told us: "Now I will have something to think about. Today is an event for me!"

"They are always talking about building prisons. But what you see here, what you learn, is that there are people who don't belong in prison. Why not start by letting them out? Then there would be room for the others."

"There are some people here in prison who can't say anything about it. Sometimes they are innocent. But if they talk, if they say aloud what they know, somebody will settle accounts with their families. They'll be condemned to death."

The group upstate, and the families, as I have already said, are an extension and enlargement of our parish at Rikers. This is not official, and no effort is made to interfere with what goes on elsewhere. We have no special privileges. It is simply done in the name of friendship, and of what we once began together. The Sisters of the Gospel, especially Amy and Carmen, have taken this to heart as their first priority. If it were not such a matter of time and of means, we would all like to go there together. We do have, as I have mentioned, *The Link*, a quarterly newsletter that marks the unity of all of us and is our obligatory and practical response to the abundance of letters we receive.

As for those who get out of prison and find themselves on the street once more, we have plenty to add to the statements one hears about need and insuffficient means, whether at the level of the neighborhood or ward, or of the city itself. Our situation enables us to see all that up close. Seeing someone back at Rikers, again and again, is a clear sign of failure somewhere. Before we get around to deploring the effects, our society is a long way from having addressed or responded to the causes: poverty, lack of education, racism, broken families, and so on. An agency or a referral can't do everything. We need people like Jacques Travers, a magnificent brother in our neighborhood, the saint of Brooklyn, who was taken away much too early by cancer. He often came to Rikers: a giant, openhearted man, extreme in his actions and in his work for the faith. He said one day: "Yes, I have eliminated authoritarianism, violence and lying from my conduct absolutely, because that style is neither Christian, nor human, nor effective." With his friends and ours from our beloved *Catholic Worker*, with Dorothy Day and Peter Maurin, he wanted "a world where it will be easier to be good." "If every family that had the means to do so would take in one homeless person, there wouldn't be a problem in New York," he often said.

Those who are suffering from AIDS, at Rikers or elsewhere,

deserve a special mention. In 1988 forty-six died of AIDS in here. AIDS victims are first in the thoughts of many people. Their unique situation makes a powerful impact from top to bottom: those who fight, who hold on to hope or who have none left, those who plunge into the incomprehensible, and those who know nothing. Many are the memories of our meetings, of dialogues without masks, of approach, refusal, acceptance. Many are the memories of friendship. "I don't need nurses —just the other sick people. We help each other." I think of Nicholas and some others who wanted so much not to die in prison. I think of this one, departing in freedom, another in ridicule. "Why do they let somebody die in prison?" To that question I have no answer.

I go everywhere, bearing the sacraments of life. I go in the church and with the church, from which I have received everything and who has sent me here; the church I cannot let go of, if I want to stay on my feet. Even with all its faults, I have always believed in its treasures.

For thirty years no profession, no function, no state of life has been in more turmoil than the priesthood. Priests are part of the world, and the world has changed a lot and goes on changing. The year 2000 will soon be here. That means adjustments, revisions, movement. And if things move, the result is often insecurity. But to refuse to move doesn't make it all right, because that only ends in paralysis. This, too, is the work of the Spirit. "The Spirit is a spirit of order and a spirit of disturbance," we learned in the seminary. You are never finished with being baptized; you are never finished with becoming a priest. I say this to the inmates, and I say it to all of us. I take part in the changes and include myself among the problems of the day, and, if God wills, as with all those who are searching for God, I include myself in some part, according to God's choice, of the solutions. No one who is with God can call himself or herself unemployed or retired.

This prison at Rikers is not my kingdom. But I agree with what an Andean bishop said: "A people and the gospel are enough for me." At Rikers, as I hope I have shown, there is a people, and there is the gospel. So I can say, without being deaf to the cries or blind to the responsibilities, "That is enough for me."

We need to talk to one another. If my readers retain nothing from these pages except that one simple but pressing invitation, it will be enough; for talking, in prison or anywhere else, is often life itself. It means killing the beast. It means keeping, in this place where its rejection is so natural, the proof of human existence. A world built solely on justice, on law, cannot replace a world of dialogue. How many times have I witnessed the frustration of prisoners who have never had the chance to explain, to tell from start to finish what has happened to them. How many know nothing of their lawyers, have never seen them, have no idea what is going on. And when they are Hispanics or others who do not understand the language, the darkness is multiplied. I am not absolving anyone or justifying anything, but how often have I seen the hate and tension melting simply because of a word, a dialogue begun even through the bars. In this house full of thunder and lightning, conversation is often the pearl that redeems everything; it means recognizing that it is only our sorrow that makes us human. It means not just "seeing" the other person, but learning about him or her and discovering something new together. It means assisting the other's self-discovery, because when we try to hide from everything, we no longer know who we are. And there are a lot of escapes here. People hate what they do not know, says the Arab proverb. We have to break the glass of separation and ignorance. There is nothing else that immediately reveals our good conscience. Even if it is far from being a solution to everything—even if it is just a good beginning—we need to learn to talk to each other, especially when we think that everything separates us. In prison, you die of emptiness and being forgotten. And if some people become animals here, it is because animals do not talk.

12

CONCLUSION

A Christian spirituality will never get beyond revolt and despair unless it takes hold of them, at least in a first and necessary movement which it must always keep in memory. The good knight journeys together with death and the devil. Job and Ecclesiastes are both sacred books.

— Etienne Borne

I place this thought, tempered by fire, at the beginning of my conclusion. It was written by one of my teachers. And I apply it to all those "knights," not all of them in prison, but all of whom have experienced some taste of the negative and of evil. And I associate it with two sayings of Jesus: "This kind [of demon] can only be cast out by prayer" (Mk 9:29), and "No one is good but God alone" (Mk 10:19).

I do not believe that there is a "normal" life anywhere — a life without problems, a destiny sheltered from choice and from risk, such as one sometimes reads about in storybooks. On our ancient earth, one day or another, everyone of us is upended, confronted, wounded. We are all in the same boat. There are relationships with the immediate surroundings, and there are others, with what is going on far away and everywhere. It is not a thing of no value, for example, that some inmates at Rikers were able to send money for the famine in Africa. There is a movement in the world, something that is pushing and to which I am called to respond where I am — because everything, whether I will it or not, is invading me. My life is no more normal than the normality of the world, no more abnormal than its abnormality. The ostrich cannot evade the storm, even with its head buried in the sand.

The word that most often occurs to me at Rikers is *exodus*. It originates in the Bible, it defines the church, it underlines a message. My unalterable status as a foreigner plunged into the brutal reality of a huge New York prison — just as so many others are here — represents a permanent invitation to be in motion, on the road, and a vital obligation to reflect, to learn everything anew. It is an antidote against stereotypes, rigidity and comfortable ideology.

Being a pilgrim means being willing to approach the treasures of a wisdom the world no longer respects; it means no longer knowing how to close one's fists. The humility, sweetness, and simplicity of the little ones are always provocations for the wise.

And never more so than in the midst of the journey, when there is nothing left but desert.

I listen to Teresa of Avila say that "all of us have only two hours to live." That is certainly no invitation to quiet resignation, to do nothing and wait, because that is the thing to do when the knell is sounding. Our world is so full of urgent demands that it has no room for the timid or the lukewarm. But in a prison it is also a good thing to know that time passes, and that all clouds are powerless in face of the sun.

I have spoken of provocation. How often, in twenty-eight years of priesthood filled with events, with faces and challenging encounters, have I been thankful that first of all I can confront, face to face and at point-blank range, my own poverty, weakness and clumsiness. It is impossible to avoid it; it is lurking in nearly every corner. These pages would have been much too polished, mutilated or even sterile if I had concealed the reality of sin, the tree of nature and all the enslavements that, except for God's transparent grace, would have remained stuck to me.

At an age when the past reasserts itself, I cannot resist repeating what the famous Father Sertillanges confided to some of his brothers, near the end of his life. I am quoting from memory: "If there are many things that I would wish not to have done, there is not a single one of them that I would want not to have experienced, because everything has spoken to me of the inexhaustible goodness of God."

Wounds do not heal themselves; they do not endure like cancer. We have to lay them before the crucified Christ. And then we have to let the psalms and the liturgy take hold of them. In every language we can say, "I will sing of the goodness of God." All eternity will be singing.

God is smart. If I were to use the French word, *malin*, it would carry overtones of "sharp, cunning" — someone who amuses himself or herself at the expense of others, someone who is a bit too sly, who profits by sharp practice. And that would be awful nonsense. What I mean to say is that, here and in the whole universe, God knows what God is doing. It is good to keep that in mind. It is written in Genesis: "I will never again curse the ground because of humanity" (Gen 8:21). That assurance is woven through all the pages of the Bible and bursts out in Jesus: "It is I. Do not be afraid!" He ascends the cross, not in order to bring about the Father's change of heart, but in order to speak to us of another way and to invite us to follow it, in the perspective of the assurance of a universe that is re-created, transformed, completely new on the day of Easter. Nothing remains except praise and celebration.

I do not know whether Assisi and New York are still confronting one another on the walls of the cinema in Montreal, without being superimposed or mixed up. This way of juxtaposing them, of being able to take in both of them in one glance, of seeking for one single music in the two of them in order to better understand and appreciate them — could it be that in order to do all this, we have to begin from some very hidden places, such as Rikers?

Someone said to me recently: "You ought to get more involved with New York, with the archdiocese. You are too attached to the Mission de France. But it's over there, and you are here!"

And I told him that what I had just been writing, these few pages scattered over time, were precisely due to the Mission. It was the Mission that invited me to give some form to the content of what I have experienced at Rikers. I think it is not a bad thing to find some brothers, at the same time close and detached, who, opportunely and inopportunely, probe us, attract our attention, set us in motion. These features we all share are our "story." And, because they are our story, they can be joined with those of others. I admit that I have been thinking primarily of the young people, especially those I have known. If I have had the privilege, more than once, of listening to young people's dreams, they also have the right to the stories of the older people; nothing remains alone, everything is in communication. And because, really, there is only one age, that one which measures itself only "by the extent of the future one has before one."

And what difference does geography make? I still love New York and Brooklyn, and I know that they have extended no miserly welcome to me. No less can be said of the seeds planted. I cannot forget. I have seen too much death and life here. The choices are everywhere, the echoes, the possibilities.

But the parish where I am is not seen, is not heard. You can even disappear there quite cleanly without the world's being astonished or stopping to take notice. It renews itself from time to time, even rather rapidly, not so much through the efforts of its pastors from outside as through the essence of the flock itself. Viewed from afar, it has no face, no interest, no future. It is over there, near LaGuardia Airport. There is also a big cemetery not far away. There is a lot of water around it. People are often forced to enter it, or are put there for all sorts of reasons. Some of them are quite strange. You can't do anything there. They say it is dangerous. One thing is sure, and you can count on it — no matter where or from which side they go in, and no matter what twists and turns they make — no one who once gets into the place will ever come out the same.

Who shall separate us from the love of Christ? Shall tribulation, or distress, or persecution, or famine, or nakedness, or peril, or sword? As it is written, "For thy sake we are being killed all the day long; we are regarded as sheep to be slaughtered."

No, in all these things we are more than conquerors through him who loved us. For I am sure that neither death, nor life, nor angels, nor principalities, nor things present, nor things to come, nor powers, nor height, nor depth, nor anything else in all creation, will be able to separate us from the love of God in Christ Jesus our Lord.

(Romans 8:35-39)